The Road to Victory

Francis J. Spellman

SEQUERE DEUM

January 1, 1943

Dear Major Bowes,—

I am very grateful to you for your graciousness and generosity in publishing a special edition of "The Road to Victory" for distribution among your friends and for presentation to every library. With very best wishes and regards I remain.

Devotedly yours

Francis J Spellman

Major Edward Bowes, K. M.,
New York.

THE ROAD
TO VICTORY

BY

FRANCIS J. SPELLMAN

Archbishop of New York,
Military Vicar of the Armed Forces
of the United States

NEW YORK
CHARLES SCRIBNER'S SONS
1942

42 — 36374

97-B2171

13306

Dedicated to the
Sweet Land of Liberty

Contents

Introduction

AMERICA faces one of the greatest crises in her history, a crisis as grave as Valley Forge and Gettysburg. Victory will not come because we the people of America wish it. It will come only if we the people of America win it. Freedom is not a commodity that once possessed is never lost. But it will be inevitably lost for us unless it is cherished, fought for and preserved in the same way in which it was proclaimed and won in the beginning.

On September 22, 1940, I had the honor to address the American Legion, assembled in National Convention at Boston. My subject was "The Road to Peace" and the vital sentence in the address was: "It is better to have protection and not need it than to need protection and not have it."

At that time the frequent and fervent prayer in all our churches was for "Peace with Justice" throughout the world. It was the prayer of peoples of good will every-where. It was the phrase and the prayer of Pope Pius XII. It was the aim and the hope of President Roosevelt.

Then with fire and brimstone came December 7, 1941. America's throat was clutched, her back was stabbed, her brain was stunned; but her great heart still throbbed. America clenched the palms of those hands oft-stretched in mercy to the peoples of the nations that struck her. America's brain began to clear. America began the fight to save her life.

Our prayer for "Peace with Justice" became a prayer for "Peace with Justice after Victory," for it was dis-mally clear that only through the predominance of American man-power and American arms could any-thing except death or enslavement ensue.

At that time I gave another address and I titled it "The Road to Victory." To the word "Victory" I gave the wid-est and deepest significance, for my thoughts and prayers are for a total victory, a victory not alone on land, in the air and on the sea, but a victory also for America's ideals. I believe this total victory can come only through religion, and I believe that through religious faith and religious life it can come and will come.

The leaders in the achievement of this total victory must be the men in our Armed Forces. They have the responsibility of winning the battles on land, on sea and in the air. They have also the responsibility of leadership in opening up a second front, "A Second Front of Prayer." This is of essential importance in winning of any victory because then we are on God's side and, therefore, God is on our side.

This book is dedicated to our "Sweet Land of Liberty," the land we love. But for the soldiers, sailors and marines, who are in the forefront of this battle for our country's life, this special edition of "The Road to Victory" has been prepared and is offered to them in grateful tribute by the Holy Name Society.

FRANCIS J. SPELLMAN

New York
October 16, 1942

CHAPTER ONE

Our God-given Rights

L ONG BEFORE the birth of our Republic, even from the very dawn of Christianity, the Church proclaimed before the powers of paganism and the tyrannical absolutism of monarchs, that all men are equal in their natural dignity, their destiny and in the right to recognition by all their fellow human beings. This philosophy of government is contradictory to the bad political creed and the worse political practices of those powers that boast that they will conquer us, and makes it indeed crystal clear that America is fighting for the God-given rights which the Church has defined through the ages.

The "credo" of the founding fathers of this country, the "credo" of the builders of our nation, the "credo" of great-hearted, great-souled America enunciates the truth that the individual has natural rights, that all men are created politically free and equal by Divine and natural

1

law, that sovereignty resides in the whole people and its object is their common welfare, and that representatives in this sovereignty are selected by the people and are responsible to them.

Yes, America fights for God-given rights, for her "credo" of religious freedom, industrial freedom, educational freedom, social freedom, freedom of speech and of the press.

America and Americans believe that any political, social or economic system which does not recognize the rights and duties flowing from the fundamental dignity of human personality, is a vicious system, destructive of democratic government.

Americans, true Americans, deplore and deprecate racism, hate, greed, violence, cruelty and injustice.

America, and we Americans, have only to look at the record and the wreckage caused by those governments who would now destroy us, to realize that the war we desired not, but to the winning of which we have dedicated all our man-power and resources, is being fought for our democratic way of life.

America and Americans have had a goodly measure of earthly happiness and unlimited opportunities to improve our way of life, including also opportunities generously embraced on many occasions to help the peoples of countries now treacherously aligned against us.

America and Americans are the beneficiaries of the enterprise and the sacrifices of forbears in gaining these God-given rights which we, their heirs, shall never, never, surrender.

I hold no enmity towards any people. Hatred has no place in my life. I love all men as brothers in Christ. But I am one of one hundred and thirty million Americans and millions and millions of other persons who are at war against any system of government that would destroy the things we cherish most.

As an American citizen glorying in this precious heritage of God-given rights do I take this stand. I recognize and honor not only the natural rights of the individual but the God-like character of his immortal soul.

Wherefore, if as Americans we are fighting the would-be destroyers of our God-given rights, as men and women we are likewise fighting against our very selves for the achievement of the innate longing of our souls, Christian perfection. The chief means to that double victory is fidelity to our religious convictions and to the teachings of the Ten Commandments. It is an important and a difficult battle but we know that men who fulfill their duties to God are the pillars of a nation at war or in peace.

George Washington realized this fact when he said:

"Of all the dispositions and habits which lead to political prosperity, religion and morality are their indispensable support."

President Coolidge reiterated this truth when he declared:

"Religion is the only source of moral power and the foundations of the nation will fall if faith is lost."

Franklin D. Roosevelt more often than any other President has repeatedly emphasized and restated it.

However, nations may be destroyed not only by foreign enemies but also by internal decadence.

Are our God-given rights also endangered by enemies within our borders? They most certainly are. Our freedoms are abused in the very name of freedom. The Supreme Court of the United States only recently vindicated one of our freedoms, the freedom of speech, against those who abused it by cursed, vicious language. The "fifth column" of the saboteurs of our factories and public utilities has its counterpart in the "filth column" of those who piously shout "censorship" if they are not permitted freely to exercise their venal, venomous, dia·

bolical debauching of the minds and bodies of our boys and girls. I am against "censorship," but that does not mean that I must condone those who wish to include among America's freedoms the freedom to kill the bodies and souls of their fellow-Americans, the freedom to be cruel, the freedom to be obscene, the freedom to steal and the freedom to spread disease. If these false freedoms come, America's God-given rights will go and America's "liberty," the most precious of our possessions, dearer to us than life, will succumb to tyranny and America will die.

Shall our liberty, our democracy, our country, our God-given rights be bombed or wrenched away? Shall blows and stabs from without or poison and cancer from within rob us of our God-given rights and destroy our God-blessed country? The answer must be "No!" Let us hope and pray, let us work and fight, let us live and die that America and America's God-given rights shall not perish from the earth.

II

From across the seas, men and women of all races have come to America. They have come not as to an alien place but as to a home. The expectation of the immigrant land-ing on these shores was to find a hospitable greeting such as one receives in one's own country and from one's own people, and America exceeded all his hopes. The welcome, for example, that New York has extended from time to time to the great ones of the earth has given it a reputation all its own. The generous heart of the city has gone out in unrestrained emotion to personages eminent in the sciences and the arts, to rulers of State, to prelates of the Church, to discoverers and to heroes of the land, the sea, and the air. These notables have been received with parades, music, cheers, speeches and acclaim.

I have read conjectures regarding which of these public celebrations was the greatest, but my opinion differs from them all. To find what is best and what is characteristic of this city—and of America—I have looked to a welcome which, it seems to me, has surpassed them all, though completely lacking in display and ostentation. The welcome that I exalt was extended to the immigrant whose number was legion, whose virtues were heroic; and it was extended not with any passing whim or emotion but by virtue of a spirit and policy rooted deep in our American democracy.

Although immigrant ships have anchored in other harbors of our country, New York City has been the chief port of entry to those brave and enterprising men and women who sought in America the priceless possessions which they could not hope to obtain in their native lands. And New York gave them a welcome, millions of times repeated, through the nineteenth century and into the twentieth, gave them a welcome not with public and formal ceremonies, but by simple admittance which opened to them the gates of opportunity, lifted up their hearts to heights of joy and power that no conquering king returning to his capital had ever known.

Yes, I place first the welcome that the unknown, unheralded immigrant received, and I draw my reasoning from the feelings that welled in his heart as the New York sky-line etched itself upon his vision, the hopes that sprang up in his heart, the gratitude that filled it, the courage that was born in it; and these were feelings that ennobled both the subject of them, and the city of haven that engendered them. There were feelings that translated into action have made this city greater and this greater country.

When I speak of the immigrants' contribution to our city and our country, I have in mind, in a special way, our ancestors whose days of toil are over and who have gone before us in the Sign of Faith. If, to this country, they brought no worldly goods with them, they brought what was better—their religion. They married and they made homes where poverty was sweetened, suffering sanctified, and love diffused, and all this through the invisible presence of Christ, Who, coming into the world when the home had decayed, restored to it purity and integrity.

To give the Sacramental Presence of Christ a fitting habitation, they built churches. No medieval artist ever gave as freely of his genius as they gave without stint of their hard-earned means to make large and beautiful their houses of worship. They built schools where Christ was learned and loved. They built hospitals and asylums where the Charity of Christ healed and solaced. In a word, they erected the Cross over all, and in all. They lived by the Cross and they brought up their children in the Sign of the Cross. By the Cross they died, and to their children and to us they left their religion as their most precious legacy.

From our fathers and mothers we have a heritage not surpassed anywhere among the children of men, a heritage for us to cherish, to defend and to perpetuate.

III

While it is true that on the threshold of eternity we are judged not by what we know but by what we are, not by knowledge in the mind, but by charity in the soul, it is nevertheless also true that an intrinsic union of knowledge and love, wisdom and charity, is the essence of Christian living.

St. Thomas Aquinas teaches, and as a matter of fact it is almost self-evident in its clarity, that we can love only what has reached us through knowledge. But imperfect knowledge can be accompanied by perfect love, which in turn leads to deeper knowledge. Thus should followers of Christ make progress in nobler love and better living. Love of God infallibly urges us to know more about God, as our Way, our Truth and our Life; and by a divine instinct it also makes us yearn to penetrate more deeply into Christian Truth.

The true Christian teacher, therefore, inspired by the impulses of the Divine Master, always remains a learner because he is a lover of God. The priest, the religious, or the layman in whom the Holy Spirit lives, immediately senses the beauty of divine truth. He desires to know more and more of Christ's teachings, and logically, therefore, he should be inspired to a more fervent and apostolic life in Christ Jesus. For, as Aquinas so sublimely expresses it, the ultimate perfection of life is "that divine truth be not only seen but also loved." No more beautiful prayer can come from the heart and the lips of a teacher than the prayer of the same St. Thomas, the Doctor Angelic:

"Send Thy meekness, O Lord, into my heart so that while I here fight for the love of truth, I may not lose the truth of love."

Not only is the world morally sick; it is also mentally unbalanced. No stronger proof of this fact can be adduced than that millions of men with every reason and every possibility to be happy and every desire to be at peace are actually and grimly calculating to destroy one another and, incidentally, to destroy themselves.

The Wisdom and Charity of God and the knowledge and love of Christ are the only means that can save mankind. The peace for which the world moans can be effected only when power is ordered by wisdom and exercised in charity.

With boundless courage and patience we must pray and work that Christ be better known and better loved. Only heroic sanctity can bring back a degenerate world to the order of charity, which is peace. One of our modern saints has said "the prayer that inflames with the fire of love" is the lever that will lift the world. This is the message of Pope Pius XI when His Holiness said:

"We have a word we can repeat as many times as we may be asked what should be done by all those who desire the good, the peace, the general concord and the general welfare of the whole Christian family. . . . Our word is that they should firstly, pray; secondly, pray; thirdly, continue to pray. . . . It is that which we do, inviting all to pray and persevere in their prayers, for it seems to us that men have until now said too much and said it too uselessly."

Pius XI was but repeating the thought of St. Paul in the beautiful words of the Apostle to Timothy:

"I desire, therefore, first of all that supplications, prayers, intercessions and thanksgivings be made for all men: for kings and for all that are in high station: that we may lead a quiet and a peaceable life in all piety and chastity. For this is good and acceptable in the sight of God our Saviour, Who will have all men to be saved and to come to the knowledge of the truth."

IV

How sad it is to think that the world, and especially our own country, has made such progress, intellectual, mechanical, industrial, and at the same time has retrogressed morally and religiously. It is a challenge that we all must face and meet with all the strength and with all the grace that God gives us.

Today the world needs the leadership of men of faith to penetrate the modern darkness. News coming to us hourly from abroad tells of men slaughtered, homes shattered and nations crushed into the earth. It seems as if we are watching the downfall of civilization. When we add to this our domestic problems of social, industrial and racial unrest, it is no wonder that many hearts are sad as they look to the future.

The forces of selfish materialism are surging ahead. The only power that can overcome such selfishness is to be found in the teachings of Christ. Yet men by the millions have drifted away from those teachings. Many who still retain some vestiges of religion are filled with skepticism and doubt.

Groping for the truth, faintly trusting, calling on some mysterious, unknown Power above, that is the plight of so many people in the world today. Our age, in the words of the Pope, has added "new errors to the doctrinal aberrations of the past." In our days, he adds, "dissensions come not only from the surge of rebellious passion, but also from a deep spiritual crisis which has overthrown the sound principles of private and public morality."

In this hour the Church stands forth as the champion of truth and as the defender of morality. In every period, there have been some who scoffed at her as old-fashioned and outmoded. They would bring morality up to date and accommodate its "time-worn" canons to the so-called enlightenment of the day. This is a criticism with which we are all familiar. It represents the extreme in an individualistic approach to religion and morality. It is the ultimate in the social, political, economic and moral philosophy of *laissez-faire*, "Eat, drink and be merry." It is morality defined by its antonym.

We should be keenly aware of the disastrous consequences of individualism with all the selfish ruthlessness it engenders. We cannot be satisfied with the policy that disregards the common-denominator interests of all our fellowmen and submits to the force of cunning and greedy minorities. This represents one extreme. On the other, is the modern trend toward a philosophy of collectivism, wherein men are but part of a mass, and simply economic or social units of the absolute state. We cannot be satisfied with the status of being cogs in a machine, regimented and bereft of freedom.

Both the individualist and the collectivist brand the Church as reactionary and behind the times. Yet truth does not lie with the extremes. It stands in the middle. The Church, the voice of truth, holds the via media. She tells us that God's law is the supreme rule of life. It must come first before everything. That law is known through the use of reason, through the inspired word and through the teachings of the Church. Under that law God has created the State.

To each one of these three, man, family, State, God has given inalienable rights of which no one can deprive them. To man, life, liberty and the pursuit of happiness; to the family, unity and autonomy; to the State, jurisdiction over the temporal welfare of all the people. But with these rights there go responsibilities and duties. The efforts of man, the family and the State must be subordinated to the spiritual destiny of mankind. The affairs of man and of society are subject to the rules of justice and of charity. These rules are rooted in the eternal will of God.

CHAPTER TWO

A World at War

THE REASON the world is at war is that the rulers of people and the people themselves have spurned or have forgotten God and God's commandments. Many of the sufferers on both sides are innocent victims, thinking and praying as we are thinking and praying for peace, a peace with justice.

We sympathize with them and with ourselves in this predicament, for our hopes and our help go out to all the suffering peoples. Our prayers are with the living and with the dead. Yet we ourselves must look to the lesson that their plight and our own plight teach that we must put our own house in order against those who through malice or ignorance would tear it down. This means that we must be vigilant against internal as well as external enemies.

When I went to school, freedom of the press meant the presentation of facts with decency and sincerity.

15

Now, there are those to whom freedom of the press means license to publish pornographic literature and to distribute it freely with the resulting corruption of minds and morals. When I went to school, freedom of religion meant just what it said. Now it seems to include the freedom to destroy religion. When I went to school, freedom of speech consisted of saying indeed what one believed to be true, but it did not include the prerogative of making venomous, subversive speeches against our form of government and the public advocacy of violent measures to overthrow it. When I went to school, freedom of assembly was not interpreted to mean the right to browbeat and headcrack law-abiding citizens minding their own business.

What are we going to do about it?

We should try to live ourselves and let others live in accordance with God's commandments and in accordance with the Constitution of the United States. As far as we possibly can do so, we should try to put God back into education, into the home, into government.

At the present time there are two very separate camps into which the world is divided.

One of these groups is striving to raise the standard of living. It is a much-used phrase and in no place is its meaning wider and more true than in the United States.

We are pioneers and leaders in raising the standard of living. In the spiritual sense, as well as in the material, no force has done more to raise the standard of living than the Church. And when I say "standard of living" I mean standard of living in all the possible phases of its meaning but especially do I emphasize the standard of living righteously, living in accordance with the laws of God, God's commandments.

In that sense not every American nor every Church member is raising the standard of living. There are also destructive forces in America. And for a juxta-phrase, I would say that these forces and these nefarious influences may be characterized as representing hordes who are "raising the standard of killing," not only of killing bodies but of killing souls.

God had been taken out of life, education, industry and political activities. Now we are reaping the whirl-wind.

When God is taken out of human life, when God is torn from the foundation of human living, diverted from the motivation of human actions, when God is supplanted by a substitute as the mainspring of human ambitions, then standards of morality are lowered and conversely standards of killing souls and bodies are raised.

II

When the combatants put down their arms after World
War I, historians took up the pen to expose the origins
of the sanguinary struggle, and many causes of the war
were listed in books that have been published in the last
two decades. By these authors the World War was ex-
plained in its beginnings by the rivalry of nations for
power and wealth, their quest for territorial expansion
and imperial domination, their seeking of new markets
and outlets for capital investment, their attempt to take
advantage of backward people, motives, all of them,
materialistic, sordid and ignoble.

If these were the underlying causes of World War I,
American soldiers knew nothing of them. These were not
the motives that stirred their minds and inspired them
with the will for victory. Theirs was an unselfish crusade.
They fought for pure and high ideals. The spark that
flamed them into patriotic fervor was flashed by the
President of the United States and they judged it their
task, whatever the sacrifice, to bring to accomplishment
the ardent hopes that our Chief Executive had formulated
in matchless sentences vindicating the inviolability of
small nations, the security of democracy and a world rid
of the threat and actuality of war. Even though secretly

mocked and later openly thwarted by foreign statesmen, these principles were sincerely proposed by President Wilson and by American soldiers as sincerely accepted.

Let historians, economists, sociologists and philosophers who explore human conduct decide among themselves the reasons for the outbreak of World War I, but for a confirmation of my recollection and my understanding of the reasons for our own involvement I need not resort to books. I turn to living witnesses, to the American soldiers; and to my query why America threw its power into the contest, they tell me as they have told their sons, that for them and for all the children of men they braved every peril that they might inherit and possess a world that would not know the evil of war, since the causes leading to war had by their determined valor been removed. For the disruption of peace, for the calamitous miseries that now again oppress mankind, for the sorrows that we fear are yet to come, the responsibility must be placed on others. There can be no revilement against the American soldier; for he took no land that had to be reclaimed, he committed no economic wrong that had to be rectified, he suppressed no political liberties that only an uprising could restore. His honor is forever secure. In military annals the American soldier of World War I belongs to the company of the most knightly who fought without fear, without reproach, and without thought of personal gain or national expansion.

III

Despite the failure in the realization of our aims in World War I we still remain idealists. To be otherwise is impossible for Americans. But experience has taught us a measure of realism. We know now that we cannot draw the boundaries of states on the map of Europe so that race will never transgress upon race. We know now that we cannot bestow our democratic institutions on people opposed by natural feelings and traditions to our political system. We know now that we cannot continue to remain unarmed when other countries have not imitated our peaceful example. We know now that it is our pressing duty to defend ourselves, our lives, our liberties, and our institutions. We know now that we are fighting World War II for the life of our country, for the life of our dear ones, for the life of our ideals, for our own lives.

What is worthless needs no guards set about it. The more valuable an object the more it calls for protection. Treasure is kept in secret vaults. A city is patrolled by police. A home is locked and barred against intruders. If in this world there were no greed and envy, no violent actions to enforce illicit desires, these precautions would not be necessary. Nations do not differ from individuals and although we have envied none, have wronged none and have coveted nothing, although we have shared our abundance with a distressful world and have felt ourselves charged to do so before God and men, we know that in many cases our charity has not been requited, our good will has not been reciprocated. We also know that our national wealth and our national way of life aroused envy in others and this envy has incited attempts to conquer us by force of arms, to take from us that which belongs to our people.

For who can gainsay as he envisages on the one hand the vast natural resources of our land and on the other hand the present rapacious temper that is abroad, quickened and emboldened by modern mechanical invention, that it would be worse than folly if we did not build ourselves strong. It is better to have protection and not need it, than to need protection and not have it, as we have learned to our sorrow.

We Americans want peace and it is now evident that we must fight for it. For other peoples have wanted peace and the peace they received was the peace of death. Our good will and the sincerity of our desire for peace were demonstrated to the extent of sinking our own battleships. We cannot longer afford to be moles who cannot see, or

ostriches who will not see, for the solemn agreements of
the black-hearted leaders of some people are written with
a blood-stained, blood-dripping finger in the blackness of
the midnight of civilization. Vices have become considered as virtues and truth has become a synonym for falsehood. We Americans want peace and we shall fight for
peace, but the peace which we want for ourselves and
the peace which we wish for others is not a peace whose
dilemmatic definition is slavery or death.

Valuable as are our material possessions, more precious still are our liberties. For these blessings, of a
higher kind, no less than for our natural wealth, are we
indebted to God. This truth was forcefully enunciated by
the Catholic Bishops of the United States assembled in
the Third Council of Baltimore in the year 1837:

"We consider the establishment of our country's independence, the shaping of its liberties and laws, as a work
of special Providence, its framers building better than
they knew, the Almighty's Hand guiding them. We believe
that our country's heroes were the instruments of the God
of nations in establishing this house of freedom."

These are impressive thoughts prompting gratitude to
God and a deeper appreciation of our inherited liberties.
For religion, which traces the sources of all our blessings
to a Divine Author, has always added its force to patriot-

ism when our government has summoned our citizens to the country's defense so that those who have sprung up at the call have felt themselves doubly inspired and doubly armed.

Of the twinship of religion and patriotism I have been doubly conscious as the Military Vicar of the Catholics in the Army and Navy of the United States. For I cannot conceive the propriety of an organization calling itself "American" that challenges the constitutionality of a bill providing that no government position in a state may be held by anyone who believes in the overthrow of the government by force. And yet there is such an organization. I cannot imagine an organization that openly teaches disrespect to the American flag and under the pretense of freedom of religion engages paid workers to go from house to house to attack the religion of others. And yet there is such an organization.

IV

By vocation I am a man of peace. I am consecrated to Christ, the Prince of Peace. Unceasingly day and night I pray and I ask my flock to pray for peace. "There is nothing to be gained by war that cannot be gained by peace," was the warning of Pope Pius XII on the eve of the outbreak of the present World War. I am a man of peace and I pray and hope and work for peace. Not knowingly would I injure anyone. I am a man of peace, but gone is my hope of building a world safe for democracy on such foundations as the Treaty of Versailles. Vanished too is the mirage of many philanthropic optimists who cherished the vision of a world united in peace and fraternal charity beneath the ægis of science divorced from religion and around the altar of Godless education. Blasted is the dream of a communistic universal brotherhood.

Science, knowledge, communism, these three great hopes of men, these three great deified abstractions, have wavered and failed beneath the pressure of human prejudice and selfishness and the spirit of cruelty and wickedness in high places. A great scientist, himself a refugee from the deification of race and blood, has stepped beyond his depth and suggested that mankind abandon belief in a personal God. That is just what men have done and are doing, and the net result is written in the bomb-mangled bodies and the decree-shackled minds of the world's suffering millions.

What is the answer? There is only one road to peace that I know of, the Highroad of Democracy, the road marked by the sign posts of the Ten Commandments, the road back to Christ and His teachings in personal life, in national life and in international life.

This is the road to peace. This is the road for America to take. This is the road our forefathers took when they lived and died for our national independence. This is the road that we shall travel if we are to live in peace, a government of the people, by the people, for the people. If through indifference or negligence, if through penetration or permeation from without or corruption or disintegration from within, it shall come to pass that some day some conqueror of democracy shall stand at the tomb of George Washington in Mount Vernon and with mock reverence and double-meaning cynicism salute our country's founder with these words: "Washington, we are here to finish your work!" God grant that I, for one, shall not be alive to know it.

v

Man's most precious treasure, human life, has become the world's cheapest commodity, and why? Because man, and the governments of man have stuka-dived into paganism, have strafed the Ten Commandments and the Moral Laws, have bombed the Sermon from the Mount.

The Apocalyptic horsemen of War, Famine and Disease are in full flight in all directions. Total wars, widening fields of military operations, widen also our sympathies with war's victims. Horrors unbelievable, devastation indescribable, cruelties unimaginable, shock us, sadden us. Dreadful, too, the contemplation of the inanity of it all, the insanity of it all. Dreadful, finally, the contemplation that germs are being propagated which will spread anew and afar the bloody strife.

War will endure until there is an end to hate and greed, until men seek first the Kingdom of God and His Justice. Man must think first to save his soul; if the soul is lost, what else will profit? This sad tragic period through which we are passing is not alone an irresistible opportunity to help our suffering fellowmen, women and children, for whom we feel a great surge of pity, but it is also a lesson and a warning to call on the Divine Physician with a prayer that His love may cure our ills and the ills of suffering humanity everywhere.

CHAPTER THREE

A Branch In the Tree of Life

*T*HE SPIRIT of the Declaration of Independence recognizes that all power with its responsibilities comes from God and this spirit is in precise consistency with Christian teaching on the Divine origin of authority and on the sacred rights of the family and the individual.

These parallel ideas and parallel ideals have come down through our history and never more clearly or forcefully were they expressed than by President Roosevelt in his message on January 14, 1939, on our freedoms.

"Storms from abroad," the President said, "directly challenge three institutions indispensable to Americans now as always. The first is religion. It is the source of the other two—democracy and international good faith. Religion, by teaching man his relationship to God gives the individual a sense of his own dignity and teaches him to respect himself by respecting his neighbor."

Yes, religion is the foundation of democracy and international good faith. It is also the foundation of national good faith and, I might add, of national salvation. Religion is not merely a word. The test of its reality is in its practice. A man's patriotism is not measured by the way he sings the *Star Spangled Banner* or how often he wraps himself up in an American flag. A man's patriotism is measured by the way in which he obeys the Commandment, "Honor thy Father and thy Mother," which implies and includes the precept to honor, love and serve one's country. I quote a sentence from the discussion of it as expressed in the Catechism:

"A citizen must love his country, be sincerely interested in its welfare, and respect and obey its lawful authority—by voting honestly and without selfish motives, by paying just taxes and by defending his country's rights when necessary."

We live in the Utopia of material progress and an atmosphere of superior intellectualism. Life has changed more in the past forty years than in the thousand years that went before, but man himself does not seem to be any better or any happier. What we understood by barbarism has been outmoded. What we understood by tyranny, cruelty and slavery has shrivelled in the wholesale light of modern efficiency in savagery and slaughter. Words have not only different meanings from former concepts but contradictory meanings.

But the Church has always taught, teaches now and will teach forever, "there is a right and a wrong in human conduct." It is the fundamental mission of every school to teach just that. The Church holds that religion and morality are the foundations of civilization. "Unless the Lord build the house, they labor in vain who build it."

To be a follower of Christ means to believe in a social rather than an exclusively individual religion. We believe that no man can serve God without at the same time serving his neighbor. That is why our Lord put the two commandments of loving God and loving neighbor together. In other words, no man saves his soul alone. Our Lord described religion in terms of a "kingdom"; St. John in terms of "life"; and St. Paul in terms of "body"—all of which imply its social character. Though the terms differ, because directed to different audiences, they nevertheless express the same reality: corporateness, togetherness and fellowship of man with man. Our Saviour did not tell us to pray "My Father," but "Our Father"; nor did He tell us to ask that "my trespasses" be forgiven, but "our trespasses"; nor did He say: "Ask for my daily bread," but "our daily bread."

St. Paul, who came to know the Church through per-
secuting it, heard a violated but risen Christ speak from
the heavens that, in attacking the Church, he was attacking
Him: "Saul, Saul, why persecutest thou Me?" Ever conscious of that social character of the Church, St. Paul
later wrote: "For as in one body we have many members,
but all the members have not the same office: So we, being
many, are one body in Christ; and every one members
one of another."

Just as the body is made up of millions of tiny cells,
each living its own individual life, and yet living the life
of the whole body, so too the Church is made up of millions of members incorporated into one body through the
birth of Baptism. And as the body is one because it is
vivified by one soul and governed by one head, so too the
Church is one because vivified by the Holy Spirit, and
governed by the one head, Whom Christ named in Peter
to be His Vicar on earth.

II

All of us then are living stones in the Temple of God,
branches of the Tree of Life, sheep in the unity of the one
fold, cells in the body of Christ, sharers with others in
the love and service of God and our fellowmen.

We do not need to go back 1900 years to find Christ,

the Son of God. We find Him living in His Church, still teaching, still sanctifying. If Christianity were only a memory of how Jesus lived and how He preached, it might hardly be worth preserving. Shall the Son of God, Creator of space and time, be limited in his power and influence to the time when he was physically present on this earth? Shall He, Who called Himself the Life of the World, be only a figure of speech for us who need His Life and His Light so badly? We believe that Christ lives in the world today as the Invisible Head of His Church, which is His Mystical Body.

There are some who reject the Church on the ground that they do not want an organization to stand between them and Christ; they understand neither the Church nor the Son of God. The fact is that the Church does not stand between man and Christ, for the Church is Christ. It was through a human nature that He came to us in the Incarnation; it should therefore be through human natures in His Church that He comes to us now. Do not all Christian religions admit that Christ gave men the power to baptize? Why do they, then, shorten the arm of God? If He could give to others the power to baptize, He could give also the power to forgive sins, the power to speak in His name, and the power to offer Sacrifice.

We believe in the primacy of the spiritual and that the

Church in teaching faith and morals will be right even though the world is wrong. We believe finally that nothing really matters except the salvation of souls. "What doth it profit a man if he gain the whole world and lose his immortal soul?" and we believe if we live in accordance with God's laws and our consciences, that we shall save our souls. If Catholics build parochial schools while sup· porting public schools, it is not because they are opposed to what the latter teach, for they both teach the same; it is only because of what is left out; it is because Christ, Who blessed the little children, who taught them and who still teaches them if they come to Him, is left out from the whole scheme of things. It is building a house or a life without a firm foundation. If we protest against divorce and birth control, it is not because we are unmodern, for these are the old practices of paganism that brought ruin to ancient civilizations and modern ones. We would like to save our country from the fate that these practices will inevitably bring about, high-minded, sincere and scientific though their advocates may be.

If we oppose atheistic Communists, Nazis, Fascists and all tyrants, it is because we disagree not only with their practices but with their philosophy. We believe that every man has an immortal soul made by God and as a sovereign person should not be completely submerged nor en·

slaved by the totalitarian shackles of any class, race, or nation.

If we seek the betterment of economic conditions, it is not because we believe that man's happiness consists in the abundance of the things which he possesses, but because human beings should have the economic necessities of life and thus be helped to save their souls.

If we love our country, it is not because it is the greatest country in the world, for we would love it if it were the least, but we love it because the virtue of piety which binds us to God is the foundation of patriotism which binds us to our fellowmen.

If hearts today are sad, if the world today is mad, it is because there is no corporateness born of the Fatherhood of God in the brotherhood in Christ. If the world today is insecure, it is because it has lost hold of the spiritual which alone will prevail when all else has failed. The Cross of Christ is the focal point of all creation. The world before Christ was a prelude to the drama of Calvary and Calvary is the perfection of love. Since Calvary, the mission of the Church has been to instill the Love of God in all hearts and in all nations. She has not achieved that mission in the world but she has done so in countless human hearts, giving them the peace of God's mercy and charity.

If the philosophy of love of God and love of neighbor had been instilled likewise by the forces outside the Church, the world would not be in the chaotic, war-torn condition in which it finds itself today.

The Church dignifies each individual and values each immortal soul. The Church teaches the doctrine of brotherly love, and obedience to God's Commandments. She opposes the philosophy and the practice of hate. That is her contribution in every country where she is free to help, where she herself has not been crushed. This will ever continue to be her mission—and God grant that it may be fulfilled.

III

Believing in God, one believes in man, in the fundamental goodness of the creature because of the absolute goodness of the Creator, in our fundamental liberties, shining as they do like flaming jewels in our frame of government, priceless and precious.

Despite the need for proper readjustments and equalizations of our economic burdens, despite the necessity of providing much greater opportunities for work for men and women who need to work and wish to work, despite the need of more hands fraternally clasped and fewer fists menacingly clenched, despite the need of a renewal in our midst of the Christian concepts of life and Christian discipline of living in which our liberties were conceived and enfranchised, despite the need of strengthening our moral fibre grown weak through prosperity and indulgence, we still believe in America, in the fundamental righteousness of our Constitution, the basic righteousness of our people in their sincere desire to live in harmony, helpfulness, and peace with their fellowmen, and in obedience to her laws and the Commandments of God.

CHAPTER FOUR

Faith Is the Lost Horizon

*L*OOKING UPWARDS to the sky in these dark nights of humanity's sufferings we seek hope in the heavens; and thence not merely a tiny ray but a whole flood of light descends upon us. On the same stars that now shine down on us looked St. Augustine centuries ago, and to his silent questioning they answered: "We are not the God whom thou seekest. He made us." Yes, the stars proclaim in luminous, inerasable language the existence of God. These stars navigate the firmament in a certain definite way, and the plan, the progress and the order involved in their movements presupposes an intelligence that could not come from matter nor from chance. And this intelligence, vast enough to regulate the orbits of heavenly bodies, we know by the name of God.

God is that same first cause who designed our bodies, masterpieces resulting from the union of a hundred masterpieces coordinated in such a manner that despite their separately complicated natures they function with an amazing harmony of action. Every fibre of our bodies, every power of our souls proclaims the existence of God, and, though other pillars upon which our lives are based may have tottered, we still have God, the supreme master of order, and firm is our confidence that through Him, out of the present turmoil, will come order and peace.

The men and women who do not lift their gaze above the present dark horizon to the light of vision from above may easily succumb to defeat and to despair. Only the soul with supernatural vision can hope to endure. Faith is the Lost Horizon, which we must find and the world must find. We cannot endure, we cannot survive in our liberties unless we use those liberties in consecrated service to hurl backwards the multiple forces of hatred, of greed and of strife, devastating and destroying the world of today. To us, who have seen the vision on the horizon, there follows as logically as night the day, the reasonableness of the consecration of our lives and our powers to keeping the knowledge of Christ in our minds and His love in our hearts.

At the gateway where our city of New York meets the sea there stands a symbol of the liberty that must not perish from the earth. Like the torch that heralded land to the eager eyes of Columbus that beacon must ever bespeak

America's vision of consecrated service to mankind. And even as the lamp of Liberty lifts its light above our harbor, so, too, is there a lamp of faith symbolized in the dark night of humanity's life by a white-clad figure who is a living symbol of the vision of a stricken but a consecrated humanity, Pope Pius XII, praying fervently and constantly and asking us to pray with him that over this poor, war-torn world of ours may yet be spread the mighty wings of God's Spirit and that all the hates and cruelties and injustices may be smothered twixt the Crucified arms of Christ.

Sorrowful millions of our fellow Americans, who are searching humbly, yet bravely, for the lost horizon of faith—sorrowful millions of their fellow human beings in other lands, may unite with us in prayer for a preparation for peace.

It is strange and difficult to think in terms of peace today at the very moment when, in the necessity of safeguarding our national interests, we are so earnestly engaged in war. Yet, essential as is the prosecution of the war, just as essential is the concomitant preparation for peace, for surely the final justification for war rests in the hope of achieving peace. No Christian can recognize the validity of war as an end in itself; no Christian can accept war save as an awful, though at times necessary, pathway to peace. Only the insane wage war or seek war as an end in itself.

I

Now if our steps are to lead us to lasting peace, we must know both where peace is to be found and the path that leads thereto. Nor need we make distinction between peace in the soul of the individual and peace in the nation, for the soul of the nation is the spirit of its citizenry, and the spirit of its citizenry is determined by the spiritual status of the individuals who, within the divinely planned setting of the family, constitute the living, vibrant units of our national life. Consequently, whatever promotes the peace of the individual soul promotes the peace of the nation, the peace of the world. Conversely, whatever destroys the peace of the individual soul threatens and impinges upon the peace of the nation.

Naturally, as a soldier in the army of Jesus Christ, I believe that preparation for peace must be in terms of the acceptance both in theory and in practice of the teaching and the authority of Christ; an application extending into all the multiple relations of men, for there can be no doubt that the maelstrom now engulfing our civilization has been created by the rejection of Christ's principles from the Councils of Nations.

There is no worthwhile preparation for peace that is not based upon the principles of justice and charity laid down by Jesus Christ. Rejecting this authority as embodied in His Church, nations have sought in vain to build their dream highway of peace. "Peace, peace," the leaders of the nations have cried, but there is no peace, for there is no readiness on the part of the majority of leaders to accept the authority and the teachings of the Prince of Peace.

Therefore shall we of America despair of the attainment of peace? God forbid! Daily we plead in humble earnestness to Our Heavenly Father, "Thy Kingdom Come," and we have the confidence born of our faith in God that His Spirit and His Truth must prevail.

We await with fortitude and also with faith, hope and charity the happy hour of peace, a "peace with justice," with independence to all nations great and small, and the protection of racial minorities. If such a peace does not come, there is no peace left but the peace of universal suffering and death.

But for the peace of life, which we work for, hope for, pray for and will die for, we must prepare by the establishment of the reign of Christ's peace in our individual souls. To that end we must be prepared for the self-imposed discipline of obedience to God's holy laws.

For obedience to God's law as expressed in the voice of
conscience is the foundation of all roads to peace. That
foundation must itself be builded upon faith. Moreover,
faith and Christian self-discipline do not contain in themselves the guarantee of peace. Charity is the binding
material of humanity's road to peace—charity first
toward God and then in God for our fellowmen in whom
we recognize His image. Charity first, last and always—
that is and will always remain the King's Highway.

Specifically, in these trying times, there is great need of
mutual forbearance, of tolerance of opinions that perhaps
are at wide variance with our own in these moments of
stress and of trial. Bigotry of race, of class and of political expedient are destructive of our peace. Let us think
forbearingly of one another. Let us be patient and con-
siderate when others fail to see eye to eye with us. Let
us remember that democracy is born of the respect for
the integrity of the individual conscience, of the individual's right to express, within the limits of decency and the
contingent rights of neighbors, his innermost thoughts and
convictions. Only by respecting the mutual rights of others
can we insure the precious heritage of our civil liberties
to the Americans of centuries yet to be. Only by charity
in all things can we assure to the future the full measure
of that peace for which the Prince of Divine Love died.

II

It is useless and meaningless to say our prayers in the morning and go forth to our work and live our lives differently from the pattern indicated by those prayers. Prayers must be not only recited in the morning and in the evening but they must be habit-forming and habit-inspiring for our lives, so that working and living, in their very essence, are synonymous with prayer, "To work is to pray" as St. Benedict says.

The present-day world has been brought to the precipice of suicide by its neglect of God, and this is because God has not been in the councils of the leaders of the world, has not been the inspiration and the ultimate end of man's actions. The dominant note of world philosophy today is destruction. As Americans and as believers in God we must cultivate in our souls the opposite philosophy, the philosophy of construction, the philosophy of building up. The first, the last, and the only way to do this is for each individual soul to contribute something that will constitute the foundation of peace with justice after victory.

Hundreds of thousands of Communions are being distributed to our soldiers and sailors. Think of what that means—that these boys of ours are living lives close to

God, realizing the importance of the trust committed to their care, realizing our dependence, the dependence of the country and the dependence of their loved ones on them. They are sacrificing their all for us and they are giving us good example not alone in fortitude and courage but also in integrity of life.

The stark necessity of sweat and blood and tears to obtain peace with justice after victory has been asserted many times, and we in our sphere of life must give more sweat for it will mean less blood from our brothers who are fighting our battles, the battles for our country's life and welfare and less tears from those mothers and fathers and wives who have given their boys to the service of our beloved land.

The New York Archdiocese has given eighty priests to serve our brothers and our sons and our daughters with our armed forces. The other one hundred and seventeen dioceses have been equally generous, and likewise the various religious congregations of men. There is no priest of the Archdiocese of New York, for example, within acceptable age limits, and having the requisite health and opportunity, who has not offered himself for chaplain service.

Eighty priests mean the equivalent of three years of ordination classes from the diocesan seminary and this contribution means more work and more sacrifices for all. Parishes have been obliged to decrease the number of Masses and make other adjustments, but it is at the present time the noblest call of our priests and a call to which they have nobly responded. In this connection, I quote a significant and eloquent paragraph from a letter which Bishop Byrne of Galveston wrote to one of his priests who had volunteered to be a chaplain, "You may make the application to be a chaplain. We have need of priests at home. No one can deny that. But if we do not win this war, our parish churches and our priests might not have much liberty to function. And so our home folks are willing to have service from fewer priests in order that the great number of our young men who have gone out to fight for us may not be neglected." And this service of the chaplains is appreciated by the men, and the chaplains appreciate the opportunities for gallant devoted service that is theirs. Thousands of letters on file in the Military Ordinariate give eloquent proof of this double appreciation and contribution. For military reasons I may not give definite statistics, but I may say that four of the Catholic chaplains have already made the supreme sacrifice for God and country; others have been wounded and still others captured with their men.

III

The City of New York and the See of New York are frequently described as "rich." What are the riches intended—the riches of material things or the riches of Divine Grace and Spiritual Power in Christ Our Saviour?

The City of New York has length and breadth and height and depth of astonishing dimensions, enclosing marvels of human invention and construction and vast treasures of wealth; and, while I am not unmoved—and who is not—by the startling evidences of size and of affluence and of progress, I do not estimate the city's pre-eminence with the eyes of one who regards only the passing external fashion. My viewpoint, as a Catholic Bishop, is the apprehension of St. Paul who wrote to the Corinthians, "We look not at the things that are seen, but at the things which are not seen. For the things which are seen are temporal: but the things which are not seen, are eternal." The ancient world had its proud edifices, but they are no more. The outward form of this modern city of New York has continually changed. Where are the mansions and the emporiums that were the glory of a former age? They have fallen before the march of time so that they are hardly a memory.

But in this metropolis there stands a building firm and indestructible, resisting the ages, and that building is the Church which St. Paul described to the faithful of Ephesus as different from all other buildings, because housing them as "fellow citizens with the saints and domestics of God. Built upon the foundation of the apostles and prophets, Jesus Christ himself, being the chief corner stone: In whom all the building, being framed together, groweth up into an holy Temple in the Lord. In whom you also are built together into an inhabitation of God in the Spirit." Where, then are we to look for the true endowment that enriches a people? Not in outward magnificence but "unto the inward man" where Christ dwells by faith and charity. Riches there are indeed in New York —unsearchable and inestimable—the riches "in the abundance of the blessing of the gospel of Christ" the riches that grace has worked and multiplied from the beginning, and through all the history of this See—the knowledge of God, piety, peace, patience, hope, long-suffering, comfort, thanksgiving, a sincere charity, and whatsoever else is virtuous to fill the heart with "the fulness of God."

I account myself only as "a servant of Jesus Christ," and I judge myself in the words of St. Paul, "not myself to know anything among you, but Jesus Christ; and Him crucified." I wear the Cross as my shield and my breast-plate because I am set for the defense of the Gospel. Armed with "the sword of the Spirit (which is the Word of God)," my mind is forward. There are as many spiritual swords as there are words of the Lord. The most invincible is the Name of the Lord Himself. The Name of Jesus sounds no uncertain call, enlists no hesitant following, promises no doubtful victory.

The enemies of God, who are by that very fact also the enemies of man, have termed religion "the opiate of the masses." I accept the challenge of that definition. The characterization is a true one, but not in the sense in which these haters both of God and man imply. Medical science has long learned to utilize opiates to lessen the anguish of tortured bodies and so, too, does religion in the nobler and truer sense bring to the tortured souls of men the restful, soothing peace of God—that union of man's spirit with God's spirit, the union of men's will with God's Holy Will, that peace that surpasseth understanding and that alone assures man at the end of life's journey of a peaceful awakening from life's "fitful slumber."

CHAPTER FIVE

Freedom to Do What Is Right

NE OF THE particular objectives of the Church should be to instruct the children of our American democracy in Christian truth and thus save them from the spiritual and temporal errors of the age. Truth and Love are opposed and contradicted by Falsehood and Hate. Truth and Love, which is charity, must prevail in our own beings and reign also in the minds and the hearts of our children.

One of the basic liberties in our American democracy is freedom of religion. It has been so from our government's beginning. The words of President Washington enunciating this principle are clear and classic:

"Of all the dispositions and habits which lead to political prosperity, religion and morality are indispensable supports. In vain would that man claim the attribute of patriotism, who should labor to subvert these great pillars of human happiness, these firmest props of the duties of men and citizens. Reason and experience both forbid us to expect that national morality can prevail in exclusion of religious principles."

And President Roosevelt in his message to the Seventy-sixth Congress repeated an historical truism when he stated that religion is the source of democracy.

Religion believes in liberty, teaches liberty and suffers for liberty; but she does not define true liberty as "freedom to do what one pleases," as anarchists do, or "freedom to do as one is told," as dictators do. Religion defines true liberty as "freedom to do what one ought to do." This liberty recognizes law and justice. It recognizes the existence of God, the fundamental and maximum authority. It recognizes individual rights and also the rights of others.

True liberty excludes the extreme of "doing as one pleases," because this makes the individual a slave of his own passions and also impinges on the liberty of others. True liberty also excludes the extreme of "doing as one must do," because this makes one a slave of other men and also a slave of the state.

True liberty is "freedom to do what is right to do," right before God and right before man. It is freedom within the law—the law of God and the law of man, which protects our own rights and prohibits us from restricting the freedom of others. We are, therefore, most free when we and others are law-abiding. Action outside the law diminishes or destroys freedom and is consequently not only a threat to government but a menace to freedom.

Therefore we should practice and explain and defend true liberty—and freedom proper to man—the freedom to do, not as he pleases, nor as he must, but the freedom to do what is right.

This concept of freedom is taught by religion. This is the American concept of freedom, freedom from the two extremes, the extreme of anarchy and the extreme of tyranny. This is the democratic concept of freedom, the American concept, the religious concept—the good of each, the good of all, with special obligation on each and every one to care for the weak, the sick and the suffering. This is the freedom I know! This is the freedom I love!

II

Youthful lives are not built by physical or intellectual training alone. Definitely will they not endure solely through health education or recreational programs. American youth needs these helps. But above all else and as a foundation for everything else there must be a belief in God, a knowledge of God's Commandments and a respect and an observance of them.

We speak of our American way of life. It is a way of life founded upon the two great Commandments: Love of God and love of neighbor. In some other lands the young are the property of the state. They are nurtured not on "the milk of human kindness" but on the venom of hate. Such a philosophy of life has changed our world into a jungle and a shambles.

What is education? Education should be the orderly and harmonious development of the God-given faculties of soul and body with a view to fitting the individual to take an intelligent, beneficent and honorable part in the life of society here on earth as a prelude to a future life with God. Its primary concern is the individual, not as a cog in the machine of industry, or commerce, or of war, but as a human being, conscious of his dignity as a man, respectful observer of the laws of God, of nature and of country, laws which in the full and free exercise of his rights as a man, he himself, in our country at least, has helped to formulate, and therefore has the obligation to obey. These are truths that should be taught in all schools: right thinking, right acting, right living; for these truths vindicate and protect, in theory and in practice, freedom for ourselves without infringing upon freedom for others.

Education should be mindful not alone of man's earthly happiness and usefulness, but also of his ultimate destiny. It appraises earthly things in the light of final values. It does not minimize the importance of man's service to the state or nation, but rather does it give to this service a meaning of incomparably greater value than is possible under any other inspiration.

Education has certain norms, the absence of which has demonstrated all too clearly the essential weaknesses of forms of education that exclude consideration of God.

Education should emphasize the objectivity of truth and as a consequence the authority of truth. Truth, all truth, whether in the sphere of the physical or the metaphysical universe, stems from God and therefore involves no contradictions. As a result the intelligent person, conscious of this harmony, reconciles the legitimate conclusions of honest science with the postulates of authority in religion.

Education, believing in the objectivity of truth, should challenge the wisdom of subsidizing the dissemination of falsehood under the guise of liberty. Falsehood, whatever its sphere, or malicious calumny, has no more legitimate claim to be freely disseminated than have the germs of disease a right to formal cultivation in the blood stream of the individual.

Education should recognize and teach that deliberately expressed thoughts, words and deeds of the individual are normal indications of character. "By their fruits you shall know them" is the succinct way in which Christ Himself expressed this truth.

III

Educators should remember that discipline is an essential part of the training of the young. Where there is no discipline, there can be no progress in education.

Unfortunately, there have been some reputed educators who, either unable to understand the nature of discipline or incapable, themselves, of commanding it, have invented an educational philosophy which, for all its high-sounding language, is a confession of defeat. Educators worthy of that name have never agreed to this philosophy of educational defeatism. The better schools have continued to function as orderly, progressive institutions, changing when change could effect a proved gain, but always holding fast to those fundamental values which are rooted in truth itself. The fact that some schools are orderly and disciplined institutions ought to make our pupils and graduates especially effective in this world crisis.

In the minds of most people a school is a place where knowledge is acquired; and indeed some can think of a school as nothing more than a factory where a product is turned out bearing the stamp "educated." There has been a great deal of discussion as to what the label "educated" really means, especially for the last two decades. Sound educators, for the most part, were sensibly restrained and objective in their judgments. They knew that they had the basic things, and that the frills and froth of some recent educational programs were not worth the discussion they provoked.

World War II probably ended all that, for already there is proof enough that by giving first place to first things, to so-called academic subjects, we were not only forming intelligent young citizens but we were providing the sort of education that the country needs right now. Our schools will therefore continue to do their splendid work teaching our boys and girls fundamental subjects and truths but they will not omit to teach the greatest truth of all, that God is the Supreme Reality, the Great First Cause, which is not only a truth to be believed but also a fact evident to the light of man's natural reason.

Teachers should continue to teach order, discipline, and respect for authority and law. They will continue with God's help and the sacrifices of many persons to give that training in all necessary subjects which prepares boys and girls for all life, life natural, life supernatural and life eternal.

In this time of crisis, we who are Catholics believe that we have nothing to change, nothing to add and nothing to subtract from our school curricula, and that our schools will continue to render a substantial service to our beloved America.

IV

The training of youth is indeed a sacred trusteeship. Good personnel, good equipment and good programs are necessary. And yet there is no training if the teaching of religion is neglected. Religion is the important element for the moulding of character, for giving purpose and reason to life. What is it that gives man the fundamental why and wherefore that enables him to rise above the utilitarian, the mechanistic approach of life? Is it not the kind of instruction that says to him, you are a child of God and all men are your brothers? Is it not the kind of instruction that emphasizes the fact that he is a person endowed with the spark of eternal life? Is it not the kind of instruction that has conserved for us the concept that man as a person created by God is accountable to God, and destined for God?

From these fundamentals flow the recognition of man's inalienable rights, and that it is the solemn duty of society to care for the poor and help the oppressed? From these considerations flow the justification of man's right to work under proper conditions with social security and the right to collective bargaining.

This is the principal concern in America today, the preservation of our personal liberties. The first official act of our Government was the solemn pledge in the Declaration of Independence to maintain and to preserve the God-given rights of life, liberty and the pursuit of happiness for all men. And for more than 160 years this Government of ours has exercised its power and authority for the sole purpose of protecting the rights, the responsibilities and the obligations that God has imposed on the soul of every citizen.

But our Government is a democracy. It is ruled by the citizenry. It is essential, therefore, that our citizenry find a sound balance between freedom of the individual and social unity. Undue emphasis on either one will lead to extremes that will be disastrous. Throughout our history, it is the Christian religion that found such a balance by emphasizing on the one hand the importance of human personality and on the other the principle of the brotherhood of man.

It has always been religion that sanctified the idea that men are important because they are persons. It has been the teachings of religion that restrain them from seeking their own selfish ends at every step of life and further urge them to consider the needs, the rights and the duties of their fellowmen. It is religion that proclaims the doctrine that all men are members of one family and children of one God.

The preservation of toleration, justice and charity depends upon training our children and youth to recognize in fellow citizens—their brothers. May the purpose of all our education be this: To make our youth good citizens of the City of God, for then it follows certainly that they will be good citizens of the City of Man.

CHAPTER SIX

A Sacred Trust

ROM the very purpose of its being the Church has not only a religious mission but also a social one. The Church's work is the sanctification and the salvation of the souls of men, and men cannot be separated from their social environment. By reason of her Divine Commission to care for souls, the Church has a primary interest and authority in both the social and economic spheres. Pius XI clearly enunciated this truth when he declared:

"It is not the office of the Church to lead men only to transient and perishable happiness, but to that which is eternal. Indeed, the Church believes that it would be wrong for her to interfere without just cause in such earthly concerns; but she never can relinquish her God-given task of interposing her authority, not indeed in technical matters, for which she has neither the equipment nor the mission, but in all those that have a bearing on moral conduct. For the deposit of truth entrusted to Us by God, and our weighty office of interpreting the entire moral law, demand that both social and economic questions, in so far as they refer to moral issues, be within the competence of the Church's concern." [1]

It is, however, as a loving and wise mother rather than as a stern authority that the Church wills to exercise her sacred ministry. She would use, she must use, this teaching authority because it comes to her as a most sacred trust. Yet in its use, from the beginning, the Church has had regard and reverence for the prerogatives of civil authorities, to whom, under the aspects of temporal interests, these same spheres of social and economic welfare pertain. From the very beginning also, as may be clearly seen in the teaching of St. Paul, the Church has conceived the human race as constituting either in fact or in possibility one mystical body, a unity both moral and spiritual, of which Christ is by Divine right the Head, and His Spirit, the vivifying soul.

Because the Church considers all men to be members of one mystical body—of one great human family—she can never approve doctrines, either social or economic, that run counter to the well-being of all the people to the special advantage of one particular class or to the disad-

[1] Encyclical: *Quadragesimo Anno*.

vantage of another. Her attitude is always that of a just and impartial mother who desires for all, especially for the weak and underprivileged, a reasonable share in those gifts with which a Most Loving Creator has enriched this earth.

II

The Church desires to be the Mother of all mankind without distinction. All men are, at least potentially, and in hope, her sons, and she will never and can never favor any social or economic group to the prejudice of others. As the Mother of all, she loves and cherishes all. But a Mother has the right, and indeed the duty, to care with especial tenderness and attention for the weaker and more needy of her children.

That is why, during the last century, when an uncontrolled Liberalism brought about an exaggerated form of Individualism, the saintly and learned Leo XIII vindicated fearlessly and clearly the rights of the laboring classes in the Encyclical, *Rerum Novarum*,—an Encyclical Letter which gave an impulse, an important and salutary one, in effecting improvements in the living and working conditions of laboring men, in furthering the ideals of social justice, in securing a living wage for workers, in asserting and maintaining the right of laboring men to organize and in having a more equitable share in the fruits of their labors.

Yet while defending those classes that are in the very nature of the case less able to defend themselves, Mother Church has never sanctioned and will never sanction a complete reversal of conditions that would make of the laboring classes in their turn either the confiscators of property or the sole beneficiaries of their labors, and deny to owners of property a likewise reasonable share in the fruits of industry and the management thereof. One evil does not justify another. Humanity is not to be bettered by the substitution of one injustice for another, or by a new form of oppression replacing a former galling yoke of enslavement, whether it be economic, social or political.

Above the shifting, contrary theories of social philosophy, and the contradictory voices of would-be social and economic prophets and dictators, the calm, quiet voice of the Pope sounds; the light of his wisdom shines forth, a beacon of truth and of reason, pointing the way to economic and social peace. Always this beacon has channeled the rational middle course of justice and peace, through the swirls of confusion.

Pronouncements of the Holy Father explain God's Laws as the natural and reasonable foundation for social life in its primary unit of the family. They are also in complete accord with the fundamental charters of our American duties and freedoms. They vindicate the right of private ownership of property but in a just manner of which the civil state is the immediate arbiter. For the right of an individual to possess property does not contravene the right of the state to restrict, by limits and conditions, the possession of that property for the common good. The right to own property is maintained by the Church, yet not without emphasizing the concomitant obligation devolving on owners to use the fruits of possession in the spirit of faith, of justice and of charity, for the welfare of their fellow-man. The Church recognizes the superior claim of the common good of all. She also proclaims and teaches the sacredness of stewardship which possession implies.

III

The dignity of the individual is of primary importance in the Church's social program. She contradicts as false the tenets of the totalitarian philosophy, which denies and would destroy the character of the individual, making almost every detail of his life, his acts and his expressions a matter of government regulation and domination. She condemns the concept of the deification of the state

or of any individual or groups of individuals who vaunt
their blood, their race, their nation, their unbridled prowess. Likewise does the Church deny the premises and
predict disastrous consequences from the predominance
of an internationalism which preaches universal brotherhood and promotes by class warfare, world-wide revolu-
tion, ruthless destruction of human life and family
life.

And what is the concept of universal brotherhood
preached by Jesus Christ? It is a brotherhood inspired
by a common faith in the Fatherhood of God, the poten-
tial universality of man's redemption and the ceaseless
mission of the Spirit of God striving to unite all classes
of people in the bonds of a true fraternity of a common
Faith, Hope and Charity.

The Church has not failed in its mission to men but men
and nations have failed to follow God. Men and nations
have rebelled against God and have cried out in the
words of Lucifer transformed into Satan, "We will not
serve."

Nations have unjustly and cruelly sought to extend
their boundaries by recourse to arms in the most wide-
spread, devastating war in history, which if it be not
Armageddon, is certainly its vestibule. The Church should
have no sword save the Sword of the Spirit. Her mission

is promoted by no other weapons save those her Divine
Founder left to her: the might of Truth and the disarm-
ing power of Charity. These are her entire armament.
Adapting herself successively, yet without compromise
in truth or in morals, to those varied forms of civil government that nations use, she carries on as best she can
her tireless and divine vocation, a Teacher of Faith,
Hope and Charity, a Shepherd of immortal souls, a
Mother of Families and Nations.

The Church, as a voice crying in the wilderness of
modern paganism, should not cease to enunciate as the
first requisite for real progress in the remaking of society,
the necessity of personal and moral reform. Without
moral standards and faithful, prayerful adherence to
those standards, men considered either as individuals or
as members of political and national groups, are but
building their own life structures, and their national
structures, on sand and on quicksand.

With sadness and with truth, Pope Pius XI gave to the
sick and dying world the healing and saving prescription
of the Divine Physician in the Encyclical, *Quadragesimo
Anno*:

"There can be no other remedy than a frank and sincere
return to the teaching of the Gospel. Men must observe
anew the precepts of Him Who alone has the words of

eternal life, words which, even though heaven and earth be changed, shall not pass away.

"All those versed in social matters demand a rationalization of economic life which will introduce sound and true order. This is the perfect order which the Church preaches with intense earnestness and which right reason demands; which places God as the first and supreme end of all created activity, and regards all created goods as mere instruments under God, to be used only in so far as they help towards the attainment of our supreme end: Peace on earth to men of good will and the eternal salvation of souls."

CHAPTER SEVEN

The Law of Love

THE DIFFERENTIATING NOTE between civilization and barbarism is love, and the law of love is still the greatest hope for the salvation of the world. Love binds together brother and brother; hate tears them apart. Love brings blessings; and the law of love, which is the law of God, brings peace. Hence we must not permit the fact of global war, which is the fruit of abandonment and scorn of God, the fruit of hate and greed, to crush the law of love, to crush civilization.

We in America are fighting for our existence, for our lives and for humanity, but because we fight, we need not hate. Rather must we by our sacrifices, sorrows and sufferings preserve what is God-like in man, for the sake of ourselves, for the sake of posterity.

How can we grow in love of God and neighbor during these days? We have the answer from St. James: "What shall it profit, my brethren, if a man say he hath faith,

but hath not works? Shall faith be able to save him?"
And if a brother or sister be naked and want daily food:
And one of you say to them: "Go in peace, be ye warmed
and filled; yet give them not those things that are necessary for the body, what shall it profit?"

So faith, too, unless it has works, is dead in itself.

Charity, the sweetest word in our language, the touch-
stone of genuine Christianity, was beautifully extolled
by Our Blessed Lord when He said: "By this shall all men
know that you are my disciples, if you have love one for
another." In the light of these words our neighbor should
be regarded as a soul redeemed and loved by Christ and
treated with the kindly love and generous service with
which we would treat Our Blessed Lord Himself. For
that reason He said: "As long as you did it to one of
these my least brethren, you did it to me."

It was the extraordinary charity of the first Christians
that helped more than any other virtue to strengthen
and extend the Infant Church. When the pagans of old
witnessed on the part of the early Christians the forgiveness of injuries, the love of enemies, the sympathetic interest in the suffering and the helping hand extended to
the poor, in a word when they learned that in the Christian concept of life all men are brothers in Christ Jesus,
they became attracted to the faith that inspired devotion

to such ideals. Our charity towards the suffering, the handicapped, and the poor alleviates sorrow and it also increases the love of God in ourselves and in others. Thus does charity contradict paganism. For deeds are more convincing than debates.

"Which is the greatest commandment of the law?" Christ was asked. Our Saviour answered: "Thou shalt love the Lord thy God with thy whole heart and with thy whole soul and with thy whole mind. This is the greatest and the first commandment. And the second is like to ·this: Thou shalt love thy neighbor as thyself. On these two commandments dependeth the whole law and the prophets."

This is the law of God: love of God and love of neighbor. All the rest of the law, and all that has been said by the prophets, flow from these two.

Between them is an inviolable unity.

The very heart of Christian civilization is charity. It is based on the unity of mankind, one in origin, one in nature, one in redemption and one in eternal destiny. It springs as from a Triune Source: the Fatherhood of God, watching benevolently over the least of His children; brotherhood in Christ Who lived and died that all might be saved; and sanctification by the Holy Spirit of Love binding men to God and man to man.

In this shattered world of ours, many are today turning anew to religion for strength and consolation. In the Church they find a secure guide to peace and justice, and a kindly Mother binding up the wounds of man. There, too, they find an ever tender solicitude for the sick, the orphaned, the old, the wayward, and the discouraged. Charity has always been her badge of honor.

The times have thrown us closer together, have forced us to realize how truly we are neighbors with so many common interests to be safeguarded, so many common hopes to be achieved. Our liberties and our free institutions are to us God-given treasures for whose protection we stand as one—strong, alert, resourceful and determined. God grant that a united America may hold aloft the torch of Christian ideals to light the way for the rebuilding of Christian civilization.

Charity binding men to God must at the same time bind Americans together in a national unity. For American charity is universal, proverbial and sacred. It is doing God's work in God's name to one of God's creatures. Charity blesses and consoles the giver as well as the recipient. Charity is the love of God in action. It is the epitome of all the Commandments. "He that abides in charity abides in God and God in him." Charity is

America's predominant virtue, charity will be America's salvation.

The Scriptures exhort us: "Before all things, have a constant mutual charity among yourselves, my little children; let us not love in word nor in tongue, but in deed and in truth."

We love our neighbor because it is God's commandment "that you love one another, as I have loved you."

In what way may we show our love for our neighbor? We may show our love for our neighbor by helping him in his needs of body and soul, by performing the corporal and spiritual words of mercy.

II

All the world's resources for succor and relief are far too small to keep pace with the destructive monster of war. As long as our hearts remain human, so long shall we continue to do our utmost for our suffering neighbors. To the question "Who is our neighbor?" Christ Himself has given the answer in the parable of the Good Samaritan. All in need and distress are our neighbors and to all should we show mercy.

In natural life as well as in the spiritual order it may happen that the victors are the vanquished and the vanquished are the victors. Certain it also is that in warfare both victors and vanquished are all victims. The innocent as well as the guilty are the sufferers. In fact, in the cruel economy of man's selfishness, of man's abandonment of God, of man's deification of self, the innocent actually suffer the most.

While no rays of hope are yet visible on the world's dark-red horizon, our trust in God must not be lessened. As St. Paul tells us, we must be patient in tribulation, instant in prayer.

We have helped all and we have prayed for all. Truly universal has been our charity as we look back over the roster of those that we have helped. Either through the Church, the Red Cross or other agencies, we have constantly and continuously responded to appeals and we shall continue to do so until the end.

Polish, German, Italian, French, Irish, Spanish, British, Belgian, Dutch, Luxembourg and Chinese sufferers have all been aided to the best of our abilities and resources. We have helped and prayed for the victims of the war in Finland, Lithuania and the Baltic countries, in southeastern Europe and the Balkans, in Spain and Portugal and in Russia and the Far East. And we must continue to help. We must continue to pray and to sacrifice. In our prayers for the victims of one country, we invariably include prayers for all the victims. In every

Mass, in every church we plead for peace and for all, and especially for peace in our own beloved country. In addition to our prayers, we must also continue our good works.

Charity is the Church stretching out a helping hand to Our Blessed Lord suffering in one of His creatures. It offers a double blessing, a blessing for those who give and a blessing for those who receive. "He that sheweth mercy to the poor," says Sacred Scripture, "shall be blessed."

The scope of Charity embraces every phase of human life and makes its beneficent influence felt wherever human want is found. In every instance it concerns itself with the individual as a child of Our Common Father and a brother human being.

Charity is dear to us all, to us who have the inheritance of the long and fruitful experience of our Holy Mother Church. We have her inspiration and her example. We know her teachings, predominant among which is a fearless defense of the poor, the suffering and the oppressed.

"Bear ye one another's burdens," says St. Paul, "and so you shall fulfill the law of Christ."

The mandate "A new commandment I give unto you: That you love one another" is from God. The motive power inherent in that mandate has transformed the aspirations, the ambitions and the ideals of men and women down through the centuries. The Church, following Christ, has always taught that mankind would be judged by the performance of the works of charity. Individuals beyond the reckoning of numbers, pondering these words and realizing their serious import, have made and are making their daily lives a stewardship of kindly, friendly Christ-like service. Countless others have realized that the vast needs of the poor, the sick, the suffering and the under-privileged cannot be met by individual charity alone. United under the patronage of the Church, and by the vow of common poverty, they have set up institutions and agencies, which are visible signs that the ministrations of a merciful and compassionate Saviour are still in our midst.

III

The motives of the Church in charity remain un-changed. The divine commandment to love our neighbor is founded in the Will of God and the needs of human nature. These will always be immutable. However, the methods by which we assist our neighbor do change. Progress in law, medicine, science and government, has meant improved methods in all fields of human welfare. During recent years much time and expense have been devoted to the development of our hospitals. Surely no one today would plan or build a hospital without first determining the technical advances in equipment, train, ing and medical practice itself. Likewise the methods in child welfare have changed in recent years.

Our child-care program is cognizant of these changes. The social well-being of each individual child is of primary importance. His present physical, mental and emotional status depends in large measure upon what life offered him in the past. It determines, to a great extent, his present needs.

All agree that the essentials, food, clothing and shelter, should be provided on a plane comparable to that of the average family home. Over and above these a medical program emphasizing prevention, under a competent and adequate staff, is essential. Recreation so directed and regulated that the active participation of every child is assured must be an integral part of the daily schedule. Education covers a wide and varied curriculum.

It is interesting to contrast the type and the manner of caring for the sick in our America with that given to the ill and the incapacitated in another land.

A short time ago, the brave Bishop von Galen of Berlin preached a sermon in which he said:

"According to what I have learned, it is a practice in

some clinics in Westphalia to draw up lists of patients who are to be transferred elsewhere as 'unproductive citizens' and afterwards put to death as 'unworthy to live'."

If one admits the principle that unproductive men may be killed, then woe to all invalids! Woe to the sick! In our hospitals and in America, it is recognized that in serving the sick, one is serving Christ. It is believed that the care of the sick is a vocation for human beings in which they may imitate the patience, the kindness and the mercy of God.

IV

I have a love for all peoples, but a special love for people who are suffering. I have a special affection for the people of France, because it has been my privilege to visit France many times and to pass many months in that country. I have lived in all parts of France, from Normandy and Picardy to the Alps and the Pyrenees. I know the country, I know the people; and, as one who knows any country and any people, I know the virtues of the French and I know also their shortcomings.

But in such times as these we think not of defects nor of faults; we think only of sorrows and sufferings, sorrows undeserved and sufferings unmerited.

As a priest I preach love. I am against the rulers of any land who preach hate and who practice hate. Such preachments and such practices are anti-religious and anti-God. I realize that the origins of this struggle may be obscure. I realize at the same time that the sufferings are very clear and very definite and very cruel. Both as an individual and as a priest, I have, therefore, most heartfelt sorrow and sympathy and love for all victims of this heartless slaughter, slaughter of bodies, slaughter of minds and also slaughter of souls.

In this world-wide sad situation the people of all lands are suffering and we are doing our utmost to alleviate these sufferings. We hope that the example of our country and the example of the Church praying for peace for all her children—for all God's children—for all people are God's children, unless they deliberately rebel against God, will finally be heeded and followed before complete chaos follows complete madness.

We pray, therefore, that the principles of Christianity, the principles of light and of reason will emerge through clouds of darkness and hate so that once more in our lifetime the sun of peace may illumine the world, so that all nations—in the words of Pope Pius XII—"all nations, even small, may have their independent national life."

CHAPTER EIGHT

The Sword Cannot Breed Peace

MONG THE TITLES given to Our Blessed Lord by the prophets of the Old Testament was "Prince of Peace." No title was more appropriate. When He became man it was a time of universal peace. On the night of His birth angels sang His praises of glory to God in the highest and on earth peace to men of good-will. St. Paul beautifully told the effect of His coming when he wrote: "He is our Peace. . . . And coming He preached peace to you that were afar off: and Peace to them that were nigh."

This blessing of peace was constantly in the mind and on the lips of Our Blessed Lord Himself. To His disciples He said: "Peace I leave to you: My peace I give unto you." Peace was the object of His teaching. "These things I have spoken to you, that in me you may have peace." Over the City of Jerusalem He wept, because that unhappy, though privileged city, would not know the things that were for her peace. On the very evening of His glorious resurrection He appeared to His apostles and said: "Peace be to thee." From His words and His works, therefore, no title given to Christ by the prophets who foretold His coming was more fitting than that of "The Prince of Peace."

The Church has preached, labored and suffered in the cause of peace. In her liturgy she prays for peace, in her Sacraments she bestows peace, and in our day her Sovereign Pontiffs, true to the traditions of the Papacy, have been appealing for peace in words which have been among the noblest utterances of modern times.

Pope Pius X died of a broken heart in the first month of World War I, which he had made every effort to prevent. "I bless only peace," was his sad reply to the Austrian Emperor who asked for a blessing on the imperial forces.

Many of the Encyclicals of his successors constantly warned the world that war would be the result of the manifold injustices which spring from man's revolt against God. Pope Benedict XV declared that it was owing to the neglect of fundamental Christian precepts that "the peace and stability of institutions and the very foundations of States," had begun to be shaken.

"There is no peace of Christ save in the reign of Christ," Pope Pius XI wrote in his first Encyclical. In 1920 with extraordinary foresight he declared that "Our heart is disturbed by many bitter anxieties; for if in most places peace is in some sort established and treaties are signed, the germs of former enmities remain; and there can be no stable peace or lasting treaties, unless there be a return of mutual charity to appease hate and banish enmity."

Pius XI, like Benedict XV, was tireless in his efforts to obtain peace and to secure peace. The desire for peace became the dominant note of all his utterances. With clear-cut vision and incisive statements he foresaw and foretold that mankind was continuing along the road to destruction.

Amid universal acclamation Cardinal Pacelli succeeded Pius XI as the 262nd Pope of the Catholic Church in 1939. Endowed by nature and grace with the superlative qualities of the priesthood, and fortified with the precious experience of an extraordinary public career, His Holiness followed in the footsteps of three Sovereign Pontiffs who had labored and died that the peace of Christ might prevail in a bewildered world. Taking the name of his illustrious predecessor, the reigning Pontiff has also taken the active place in world affairs that characterized Pius XI. In the years that have elapsed since his coronation Pius XII has offered vigorous, positive and righteous programs for a peace with justice and charity in this war-stricken, war-saddened world.

Pius XII was destined by God to preside over the Church and to guide the spiritual destinies of peoples at a time when all the evils condemned by preceding Pontiffs were to bring forth their most bitter fruits of cruel disastrous war, a war which is, as indicated above, the culmination of the weakening of the foundation of the moral and religious ideas and ideals on which our civilization has been built. In the seventeenth century the Catholicity of Europe was shattered by the breaking up of Christian unity. The rejection of the supernatural and the inordinate glorification of human reason came in the eighteenth and the nineteenth centuries. And we of the twentieth century are witnessing the enslavement of man by the state, the cult of force, the deification of power, and the domination of right by might. Back once more the world has tumbled to the abyss of paganism and savagery. Christ and Christianity, humaneness and decency, truth and honesty have been swept aside.

But man must worship something. If he rejects the God Who made him, if he rejects the great First Cause, the Cause of Causes, he must replace Him by a god of his own invention. It may be the idol of the state, of greed, of avarice, of pride, of lust or of any created thing. It makes no difference; the result is always and inevitably the same; corruption of human hearts, strife between classes and war among nations.

II

When Pope Pius XII took up the work of his peace-loving predecessors, he employed all the resources of his office and made every possible appeal and contact to avert the catastrophe. When his noble efforts failed and the storm clouds burst with the rain and the hail and the havoc of war, His Holiness dedicated himself to the mitigation of its tragic results. Nothing has deterred him from the fulfillment of his mission as the Vicar of the Prince of Peace. At the beginning of his Pontificate he issued an Encyclical Letter addressed to all the world expounding forcefully the eternal principles of justice, charity, liberty and peace.

"The sword," he wrote, "cannot breed peace; it can only impose the terms of peace. The forces, the influences that are to renew the face of the earth must spring from men's hearts."

Again and again he raised his authoritative voice and wielded his expressive pen to expose and condemn the evils that have led to the present world distress. Against the pagan gospel of the deification of the state he wrote:

"Whoever considers the state to be the end toward which all is directed, to which all must bow, is of necessity an enemy of all true and lasting progress."

He has pleaded for the poor, espoused the rights of the unemployed and the underpaid, embraced with the immense charity of the Church the whole human family without distinction of race or rank or of color. He articulated the thoughts and desires of all mankind when he pleaded: "The whole human race hungers for bread and liberty, not for steel." Yes, and the whole human race hungers also for peace, peace for the individual, domestic peace, national peace, international peace. But no dictionary of Christian words and, I may add, no dictionary of American words, defines peace as a synonym of either murder or suicide.

The Holy Father prays and works for peace, for internal peace based on the laws of fraternal and universal charity and justice, for external peace which requires the preservation or the restoration of the rights to national life and of independence.

Truthfully and beautifully did His Holiness say on the first anniversary of His coronation:

"It is peace which is founded on the knowledge of God and of Our Lord Jesus Christ—'The way, the truth and the life'—which is the most profound wish and aspiration of Our Soul. It is peace which prompts us in our love for men, for all men, which we carry in our heart, for both those who are near to us and those who are far away, those who are faithful to us and those who are separated from us, those who are at peace and those who are at war, for it is to all that we owe the services of truth and the charity of Christ."

And this is the same peace which all men of good will desire and for which they are earnestly praying and fervently working, and I mean all men of good will of all nations.

In a world at war I believe that the desire for peace on the part of all people was never greater. This desire in its deepest source springs from religion which teaches men to love one another, and its existence is the only good augury in this sad, mad world. It means that people fear that any attempt to redress the wrongs of the world by military forces will fail lamentably as they failed in the last great war, and that future wars will arise to mock our illusory hopes and efforts.

Yes, I would have America a powerhouse of democracy and of freedom. But whence the generation of this power? From man, proud, self-contained and trusting only in himself, or from God operating with His grace in the hearts of men of good will? And what power? An idealism expressed in abstractions that have become suspect as deceitful catchwords with often contrary and contradictory meanings, or the plain, sincere, moral doctrines of religion as set forth in the Ten Commandments and the Sermon on the Mount with God their Author and Christ their Teacher? And how can this power make its contact? By reaching the minds with new forms of education based on naturalism or skepticism, or by confronting the conscience of man with his inescapable duties to God and his neighbor?

The victory that is to change the face of the earth must come from the onward march of Christian soldiers dressed as St. Paul puts it, "in the armour of God." And the armour of God is not in the ancient equipment of breastplate, shield and sword, nor in the modern implements of bombs, tanks and airplanes. In the Apostle's enumeration, the spiritual weapons that will overcome the enemy are truth, justice, the gospel peace, faith, the hope of salvation, the word of God.

The heart of the Holy Father is filled with sorrow and crushed with the suffering and the miseries of all his children in all the countries of the world. Our griefs are his griefs; our losses, his losses; our crosses, his crosses; our hopes, his hopes; our prayers, his prayers.

These thoughts are for our comfort and for our encouragement. And for our spiritual solace, be it also considered that from the heart of the Holy Father to the hearts of all his children throughout the world there come the messages and the exemplification of spiritual conformity with God's Will, of courageous fulfillment of our duty to God, to country and our fellowman, of mutual love for one another. These are the only influences that will renew the face of the earth.

From the heart of the Supreme Shepherd of Christendom in this tragic hour, when mankind is bleeding to death with self-inflicted wounds because the knowledge and the love of Christ are not the prevailing norms of human, racial and national conscience, our Holy Father, by his prayers, sacrifices and paternal love, intercedes for God's children, all of them, that we may have the grace to be, to act, to live, to die in accordance with the divine pattern given to us by Christ, our Brother, our Redeemer, our Saviour.

To our Holy Father, American Catholics give their gratitude, their love and their prayers. They reciprocate prayers with prayers and love with love. They implore the Holy Spirit to continue to bless the Holy Father, to bestow on him every gift of wisdom and grace needed during the catastrophic eclipse of charity, justice and sanity.

III

From Peter to Pius there is a continuing story of high moral courage in defense of truth, justice, charity and peace, the four words that frequently recur in all Papal pronouncements. The Popes have consistently and fearlessly preached that might and right are not interchangeable terms. They have taught that truth has objective value which both men and nations must recognize. They have proclaimed that the weak have inalienable rights which must be respected by the strong.

These words are true in an especial manner of Pope Pius XII, who possesses the attributes of many of the most distinguished successors of St. Peter, the nobility of Leo the Great, the courage of Gregory VII, the learning of Benedict XIV, the kindliness of Pius IX, the culture of Leo XIII, the pastoral zeal of Pius X, the acumen of Benedict XV and the firmness of character of Pope Pius XI.

Since Cardinal Pacelli became Pope Pius XII he has faced the colossal mission of bringing back a chaotic world to Christ and His teachings. A superhuman task in any era, it has become more so in the tragic times of the most brutal war in history.

No force and no circumstance, however discouraging, has deterred him from the resolve announced in his first Encyclical Letter, *Summi Pontificatus*:

"We shall not allow diffidence or disagreements or rebuffs to interfere with our undertaking. We shall not be deterred by fear that others will fail to recognize, or will distort our motives."

Before the outbreak of war, he did everything to avert it. After his noble efforts had failed and the forces of destruction and death broke loose, he left nothing undone to alleviate suffering and to pray and to prepare the way for peace. His manifold pronouncements have become lights from Heaven piercing the gloom of the darkest days of history. He struck at the roots of totalitarianism when he said:

"Whoever considers the state to be the end toward which all is directed, to which all must bow, is of necessity an enemy of true and lasting progress."

He brightened the hopes of the man of toil when he wrote:

"You cannot without injustice refuse to workmen the same freedom of association which is enjoyed by their employers."

And he revealed the anxiety of countless hearts when he pleaded:

"The whole human race hungers for bread and liberty, and not for steel."

His Holiness has frequently, emphatically and courageously presented the sacred aim of his Pontificate and the authoritative position of the Papacy for the betterment of a war-ridden world. He has enunciated the vigorous, positive program of the Church in the furtherance of world peace and civilization that those who guide the destinies of nations would have the vision to see and the courage and the humaneness to follow that program.

The tradition of spiritual fearlessness of the Popes, carried on by Pius XII, stands out as a torch against the darkness of the world's night. His type of courage does not mean the absence of fear but rather the conquest of fear held captive by a will that is rooted in God. The Holy Father made an analysis of courage in addressing the Religious of the Sacred Heart:

"Heart means courage and strength which are put at the service of right and justice. Heart is also pity towards the feeble, a tenderness which bends towards misfortune, forgiveness which surpasses the guilt."

Yes, Pius XII is the embodiment of spiritual fearlessness, a vital and vocal bulwark of principle against expediency, conscience against convenience and right against might.

I V

Our President and our Holy Father have combined the forces of our great country, and the forces of religion in a battle for peace, that peace which the world itself does not know how to gain for itself; that peace which can come only from the Prince of Peace.

We can do our part to further the program of peace to strengthen the forces of the nation and the Church in their moral battles for peace. By sacrifice, and by prayer, by the personal sanctification of our own lives, we can implore Almighty God to open the minds and to soften the hearts of those who have the power over the peace of the world.

I know that, humanly speaking, peace does not seem possible soon; but I know, too, that that same power that miraculously opened the ears of the deaf twenty centuries ago, that same power which has been working miracles down through the years, even to our own times, that same power is still available, and if by our lives, by a crusade of prayer, a crusade in which our Holy Father asks us to join, a crusade in which in their hearts, if not with their lips, the peoples of the suffering world are joining, then God can do and will do what is humanly impossible and permit peace to come to this troubled world.

So as Americans we should pray for peace. And the first prayer is action in sanctifying our daily lives, in remembering that we must observe all the commandments all the time, in remembering that we must realize that God is in his Heaven not only Sunday but every day, in realizing that God watches us, that God harkens to us and God judges us not only at the time of our morning and evening prayers, but all through the hours of the days and the years.

We should bring our hearts close to the heart of the Christ-child, joining with our fellowmen of good will, our fellow Americans in prayers for peace, bearing in mind the five points that the Pope has enunciated, five intentions for which all people of good will can pray:

First: a guarantee of the independence and the right to exist of all nations, great and small.

Second: a release of all nations from the slavery of armaments.

Third: reconstruction of international institutions.

Fourth: satisfaction of the fair demands of minorities.

Fifth: and this is important, that the leaders of all

nations must faithfully observe their pledged word and observe international pacts.

With the Pope and with our President, with the Church and with our nation, we can participate with our prayers and with the proper living of our lives in beseeching God for peace, peace in our land and peace for our neighbors everywhere.

v

The world has been living through dark days, darker because the potentialities for evil are greater, hatreds are deeper-rooted, and the spirit and the capabilities to destroy lives and morals are more rampant and more widely devastating. The powers of darkness have cloaked the greater portion of the world. But notwithstanding this predominantly black situation we have not been nor can we now be defeatists or pessimists. Imprisoned, crushed or martyred though we may be as our brethren in other lands have been, we are still triumphant. Reviled, calumniated, maligned though we may be and as our brethren are, we are still optimists.

As the Holy Father said:

"Our happiness does not depend solely on external events. The Church continues as the protectress and herald of faith and of morals and that is her only interest and her exclusive longing to convey through religious, charitable and educational channels to all peoples without exception the values of Christian life and of Christian living."

The Holy Father enumerates five indispensable prerequisites for Christian living and for Christian peace:

1. Triumph over hate—which is today a cause of division among peoples and races.

2. Triumph over distrust—which renders sincere agreements impossible.

3. Triumph over the principle that might makes right and the repudiation of the principle that utility is the basis of right.

4. Triumph over economic conditions which deny a proper standard of living for all.

5. Triumph over the spirit of cold selfishness which in its power disregards both national and human rights.

The very darkness reveals the brightness of the star of faith, hope and charity which is the essence of religion. This light reveals how true it is and how sadly it is true that man has failed to be true to Christ's teachings. God has not deserted men even though men have fallen away from God. Despite the errors of their ways, God, the Creator, loves and cherishes his rational creatures with an everlasting love.

Approximately twenty-one million Americans who are Catholics and many other millions of men and women of good will who believe in God and who believe in peace with justice, share with gratification President Roosevelt's action in having sent a personal representative to the Holy See with the rank of an ambassador, in order that "parallel endeavors for peace and the alleviation of suffering would be assisted." "Peace with Justice" is the motto of Pope Pius XII. "Peace with Justice" is that for which all peoples of the world devoutly yearn and pray. Full of faith and hope and warning were the words in the message of the President saying that "unless there is some trust in a Divine plan, nations are without light and peoples perish." In interpreting the feelings of his fellow citizens, the President told the Holy Father that "the people of this nation know that only by friendly association between the seekers of light and the seekers of peace everywhere can the forces of evil be overcome."

Catholics, Protestants and Jews can concur in that expression, and be heartened at the collaboration of a union of endeavor, if not in belief, of all those who are on the side of right and justice. To quote the words of

Pope Pius XI, given on March 19, 1937, we may include in this category, "all those—and they comprise the overwhelming majority of mankind—who still believe in God and pay Him homage."

This action of our President—the President of a people that believes in and that defends freedom in the practice of religion, freedom in the dissemination of truth, freedom of assembly and freedom of trade—was generally, generously and gratefully approved by millions of men of good will. However, there were some persons who did not understand this collaboration of the two greatest influences for peace in the world, the spiritual leader of three hundred million souls and the freely elected President of our nation of more than one hundred and thirty million souls.

It would seem that good will and reflection on their part, both of which are readily assumed to be present, should persuade them to be more cooperative for the purpose of "warding off from mankind," in the words of Pope Pius XI, "the great danger that threatens all alike—in order that the enemies of religion may not attain the goal they have so loudly proclaimed to the world." All should realize that without God and without religion there can be no peace.

The only reason that the non-approvalists seemed

to have for their position was the shibboleth of separation of Church and State. With the conviction that these good men would like to be informed, I shall simply enunciate the Catholic principles in this regard.

The immediate goal and object of the Church is the supernatural sanctification of the souls of men.

The immediate goal and object of the State is the temporal welfare of men, also in the moral order, and this is obtained by adhering to the principles of justice, supplying for the deficiencies of individual persons and families.

Now these objects may and do overlap since it is obvious that if the Church strives to make men better spiritually, they should be better civically and morally. Conversely, the state promoting the welfare of society works indirectly for the sanctification of souls. But this was true in 1797 when Sartori represented the United States, and it was true during the ensuing seventy years until the American mission to the Vatican was discontinued in 1867. And it was true during the subsequent seventy years, and it will still be true now that a new Ambassador has been appointed.

The Holy Father is not alone the supreme head of the Catholic Church. He is also head of a Sovereign State. Thirty-eight countries have representatives at the Holy

See. Nobody protests because President Roosevelt has an ambassador to Great Britain, even though King George VI is the head of the Church of England. The heads of other countries are also heads of religions in those countries, but no protests are voiced. Because we sent ambassadors to the Emperor of Japan, who claims descent from the Son of Heaven, there was no one thoughtless enough to suppose that the appointment meant a union of the Japanese religion and the United States government.

It may also be recorded here that one of the first sovereign states to recognize the United States after the Revolutionary War was the Papal State, and this when the separation of Church and State was recognized as an American principle.

The Papacy's service to peace among nations has long been recognized even among those who did not believe in the Catholic Church. Thus, Bismarck, a Lutheran, in October, 1885, asked Leo XIII to arbitrate the dispute between Germany and Spain over the Caroline Islands. And, speaking of a Lutheran body, we might mention the action of Finland at the time of Russia's attack upon that country. Ninety-six per cent of the Finlanders were Lutherans yet their Government expressed its gratitude for the contributions and sympathy received from the Catholic Church.

It is not necessary to inform an American public about the personality and the virtues of Pope Pius XII. The world has already drawn its own clear portrait of his character. Serene, humble, devout, sympathetic, a man close to the people and close to God, a high priest after the pattern of Jesus Christ, this was the superb figure whose appearance before the people in St. Peter's Square after his elevation was greeted with jubilant cries that were taken up with increasing volume all over the world.

No little of this acclaim rose from the people of America, irrespective of creed, of race or of class. Americans had given the then Cardinal Pacelli a glad and admiring welcome when he made his memorable visit to the United States. He who is now the Holy Father entered New York from the ocean's door, passed through our streets, looked down from above upon the towers that reached up to him, spoke to us, knelt in prayer in our midst and blessed us. These experiences and more have ratified between the Holy Father and all of us a deep and a solemn pact of mutual understanding and of friendship. How heartening to all of us to think that he knows us as we know him, that he loves us as we love him, that we can depend on his learning, knowledge and affection to aid us in our difficulties, as, in his trials, we shall stand with him in true and unswerving devotion.

CHAPTER NINE

Two Anchors — Patriotism and Religion

WHILE it is true that there is no need of any formal assurance that religious groups or bodies are at all times and in every way determined to support our government in this present emergency, still it does make us feel proud and determined to assert and to reaffirm our determination to defend our beloved country to the very limit of our resources and lives. For it is not alone a duty but it is also a privilege to place all our agencies and hospital facilities at the disposition of the Government of the United States.

This dedication does not mean any change in policies, for at all times work for the welfare of our country and for the welfare of humanity is done in the name of God. Some have the care of the sick, others have the care of the old, others have the care of the young, and this care is given in the name of Christ to whose service their lives are consecrated. People are not only willing to give their lives for God and country. They are also willing to live their lives for God and country.

I am naturally proud to know that the religious and charitable agencies have so much to offer to our government and pleased that we are so well organized. What we do as patriots, we do also for religion, because religion is the foundation of true patriotism.

I read a statement recently attributed to a retired army officer in which he said that morale is the important thing in the army and that morals are not important. This utterance is not necessarily traitorous, but its author would at least be guilty of a dis-service to his country because morale, real morale, is founded on morals. "Morale" means courage, readiness to serve, high purpose. "Morals" is that sense of right and wrong, divinely taught, courageously followed, conscientiously lived. Both serve the same cause. Morale makes a man strong in his duty to his country. Morals make a man strong in his duty to God. The man who would advocate morale for the army and rule out morals would take from morale the strength, purpose and inspiration that religion has always contributed to patriotism.

Blended together, these two forces of morals and morale form a bulwark of national defense and personalize that union of religion and patriotism which is a tradition of our Church and Country.

Religion and patriotism support, strengthen and complement each other. Without religion and its moral standards, patriotism can be made a cloak for infamy. With religion and its moral standards, patriotism has a foundation, a strength and a permanence that comes from God.

In the storm that has struck America, the ship of state will be held firm by two anchors—religion and patriotism.

So we do not begin our service to our country but we do rededicate and reconsecrate ourselves. With our morale builded upon morals, we take our places in the ranks beside our soldiers, sailors and flying men, beside the mothers and fathers, wives and children of our country's armed defenders who, like ourselves, have builded their morale on morals and will base it there till the end.

Rectitude is the only true guarantee of life even if lost, of liberty even if sacrificed, and of happiness even if transmuted into suffering. This is an assertion that needs no demonstration, no documentation.

How increasingly dark, year by year and day by day has been the sky above us? And the trend is still toward darkness. None of us can become calloused to the cruelty, the injustice, the inhumanity of it all. No matter how much we read and meditate and suffer, the thought of the futility of it all, the insanity of it all, is uppermost in our minds. But our sacred incentive is that our government and our people did everything possible to avoid the war, to promote international good faith and good will almost beyond reason.

Unfortunately, among the world's leaders many have the vices of cruelty, of hatred, of selfishness, of avarice; and we who are striving to promote rectitude in ourselves, rectitude in the young, rectitude in our neighbor, are the victims of this sad, incredible situation.

It is said that we have made more scientific, intellectual, industrial progress in the last forty years than in the previous thousand years. But I would say that during the last forty months the world has plummeted to an abyss of moral degradation never before attained or imagined in history.

What is to be done about it? We are powerless, except to carry on as we are. We must not lose courage. We must do our day's work, every day in the presence of God. We must observe as well as believe in the Ten Commandments of God.

We boast of being a civilized country, and we have

definite and sacred references to God and to religion in our Declaration of Independence and in our Constitution. But it is not enough to have religion mentioned in documents. Religion must be lived. In our lives, by our lives, by our example, and by our works and words, we should try to rebuild the strong wall of righteousness, so that in God's mercy we may block the avalanche that is sweeping humanity to destruction.

With prayers on our lips and in our hearts, we ask God's blessing on us all, on our families, on our works, on our neighbors, on our country, and lastly on our neighbors in all the world who have the same fundamental and rudimental feelings and aspirations as we have, for they would wish to love God and serve Him if they were permitted to do so.

Every nation to be successful in any veritable Christian sense must have resources not alone of material things, but also, and more so, resources of moral strength. These resources of moral strength have their fonts in those persons who have the vision of a higher and fuller life, who have a practical idealism which keeps the national attitude on a higher level than the naturalistic, who have the vision and the grace to make the all-engrossing consecrated interest of their lives the service and the welfare of others.

II

From many sources there comes the prediction that the future will be far different from the past. Any old order or any new order, if it is to endure, must not ignore the origin, the dignity, the rights and the destiny of man. Church institutions teach and exemplify love of God, love of country and love of fellowman. These three loves are essentials of religious doctrine, and we believe also that they are foundations of American democracy.

We know our obligations to our country. Gladly do we fulfill them and render our full contribution to the upholding and upbuilding of democracy. As loyal, patriotic, American citizens we have apprehensions of dangers to democracy, dangers from our avowed enemies beyond the confines of our land, and dangers from those within our borders whose concept of democracy is an arsenal of privileges for themselves.

This is a situation which evokes an important consideration. Before this present world war, and for some time preceding it, there were approximately 30,000 fewer French inhabitants in France each succeeding year. During the past decade in the United States the number of persons over sixty years of age has increased almost one-third, which is a great tribute to our doctors, to our scientists and our government. But what is vitally ominous is the fact that the number of children under fifteen years of age decreased and the trend is such that within the next generation there will be more people in this country over sixty years of age than there will be children under fifteen years.

This reflection and others of like import are pressingly ominous challenges to the domestic life of our nation. And they are challenges to our national life, for we cannot win the war for America if we lose the battle for the cradle!

Great as are our resources and our abilities it is nevertheless impossible for Americans to construct as much and as fast as the rest of the world can destroy. In other words, the powers of destruction are in the ascendant. When we think of what America has done, what medicine has done, what the arts and sciences have done to prolong life, to lessen sufferings and to make this world a more happy place in which to live, it is most pathetic to contemplate world-wide havoc wrought by demons in human form.

We offer our works of charity, in union with our prayers, that God may permit us to assuage in some degree the sorrows and sufferings that now are afflicting humanity.

III

The concept of reparation is based on the idea of the sacrifice of the individual soul even though the individual be a member of a family or of a community.

Christ's supreme sacrifice was a personal sacrifice offered by Him as head of the human race and the first One of many brethren. Christ represented the human family but the validity of His sacrifice rested on the personal element. His sacrifice was superabundantly sufficient because it was the sacrifice of a divine person.

Both reason and Holy Scripture confirm this statement. The divinely-given freedom of the will, by which in a sense man shares in the very creative activity of God, and his divinely-mirroring intellect, must both concur in the activity of the individual soul, if that activity is to be worthy and valid in the sight of God.

This is why St. Paul could write to the Christians of the early Church:

"I beseech you therefore, brethren, by the mercy of God, that you present your bodies a living sacrifice, holy, pleasing unto God, your reasonable service. And be not conformed to this world: but be reformed in the newness of your mind, that you may prove what is the good and the acceptable and the perfect will of God."

In the same vein of thought the first of the Apostles, St. Peter, exhorts us:

"Be you also as living stones built up, a spiritual house, a holy priesthood, to offer up spiritual sacrifices, acceptable to God by Jesus Christ."

From these thoughts come the most consoling conclusions, etching deeply into the tablets of the mind the dignity of the individual, contrasting and contradicting the prevailing and predominant philosophy that man and the children of man belong to the state. Religious philosophy teaches that every man, no matter how obscure his existence and his limitations in human endowments, may glorify his God and console the heart of his Redeemer by utilizing the opportunities that grace suggests and worship supplies.

Only love can vanquish hate, only faith can conquer paganism, only hope can dissipate despair; and hearts and souls must have faith, hope and love in order to live.

I V

Our duties in the face of world misfortune are two-fold: patience in our own troubles, kindness in the troubles of others. Charity partakes of both patience and kindness.

Human minds are unable to encompass the magnitude of world devastation, desecration and desolation; human hearts are unable, even in their bursting, to feel an infinitesimal part of the pain. Nevertheless, we must strive in our thoughts and in our love to be all that we should be, and to do all that we can do for the love of our neighbor, for the love of God.

Suffering we must bear with unconquerable souls. "Charity is patient," says St. Paul, and to understand and accept this truth, we must take the view of faith and eternity.

Suffering is a great teacher, and to all of us it comes in one form or another, reminding us of our weakness and our need of God and recalling that we are really exiles and travelers not yet come to our true country. Patience produces moral and spiritual power, reinforces our spiritual energies, helps us to victory over ourselves.

Eighty years ago a beautiful and inspiring patriotic song was written, *The Battle Hymn of the Republic*. One line of that patriotic hymn reads: The Lord "has sounded forth His trumpet that shall never call retreat." And another verse calls out: "As He died to make men holy, let us die to make men free." Christ died, not alone to make men holy; Christ died also to make men free, and Christ lived to make men free—to make men free first of all from sin, which is the one evil from which stem all other evils.

Our men and women are living and dying to keep America free. We, too, should live and die to keep America free, to keep ourselves free in the true sense of the word—free to do right, free to live right, free to be right, free to die right.

CHAPTER TEN

The Two Battles

E FACE two battles, the battle of life and the battle for our country's life. We must win the battle of life, which is the battle for our souls' salvation, and we must win the battle for our country's life, the battle for the soul of America. For when we say "America," we mean not alone "her rocks and rills, her woods and templed hills," we mean also the pulsing men, women and children who are the inheritors and the trustees of her liberties,—her vital, vibrant liberties sprung from the mind of God, based on God's eternal laws, embodying rights and duties for all, proclaiming freedom and justice for all—liberties enshrined in the hearts of all Americans.

Not alone of mind and body is man composed. He has also an immortal soul, which gives him life.

President Roosevelt has described America as a

"God-fearing, courageous people, which throughout its history has put its freedom under God before all purposes." This definition has an important meaning for our armed forces for it was written in a message to the members of the American Expeditionary Forces on March 31, 1942.

Therefore, mental and physical prowess are not in themselves sufficient endowments for America's fighting men to be faithful to the full import of that message as "they bear with them the hope and confidence, the gratitude and prayers of their families, their fellow-citizens and their Commander-in-Chief." They need also high spiritual resolve, for they constitute the spearhead of defense for this "God-fearing, courageous people." In war and in peace they are our strength against disintegration and defeat, against the decay of men which is just as threatening as enemy onslaught.

If America is to remain the America whose founding fathers declared that "all men are endowed by their Creator with certain unalienable rights, among which are life, liberty and the pursuit of happiness," if America is to remain America of the four freedoms enumerated in the First Amendment to the Constitution—freedom in the exercise of religion, of speech, of the press and of assembly—if America is to endure in Lincoln's words as a "government of the people, by the people and for the people," then we must keep God in Americanism, for Americanism without God is synonymous with Paganism, Nazism, Fascism and Atheistic Communism.

"Duty, Honor and Country" are our watchwords, and duty, honor and the service of our country await us.

Our duty is to win this war against the powers of darkness and to win the peace that follows it, a "peace with justice after victory," as the prayer is phrased in the Archdiocese of New York.

It will be our honor to have a part in this victory, a victory not alone of arms over the forces of those who would destroy us, but also a victory for the freedom of righteous people everywhere, because again in the words of President Roosevelt, "the vast majority of the members of the human race is on our side. Many of them are fighting with us. All of them are praying for us. For in representing our cause we represent theirs as well— our hope and their hope for liberty under God."

Our love of country and our devotion to the principles for which she stands, principles of freedom, fidelity and fortitude, have become part of us. Our faith and our love of God have likewise animated, guided and guarded us. In the union of love of God and country is our strength, the strength that will enable us, come what may, to win both battles, the battle for the eternal salvaion of our immortal souls and the battle for the triumph of our nation.

It is only a spiritual America that can win a just peace after it has won a justified war. It is only a spiritual soldier answering the call to arms of our country who can also answer the call to the arms of Christ on the Cross.

11

Because I wish to emphasize the spiritual element in the lives of soldiers, I would consider them as missionaries as they depart to their posts in distant lands in conquest of souls for Christ. I would quote a most humanly and spiritually touching letter, a letter found among the possessions of a young Royal Air Force Pilot listed, "missing, believed killed." His commander read it and obtained permission from his mother to publish it anonymously under the title, *An Airman's Letter to his Mother*—"The Fight with Evil—My Earthly Mission is Fulfilled." This letter will bring us all closer to God and the recollection of it will keep us there: *

* Published as a gift book, copyright by E. P. Dutton & Co. Quoted here by arrangement.

Dearest Mother:

Though I feel no premonition at all, events are moving rapidly, and I have instructed that this letter be forwarded to you should I fail to return from one of the raids which we shall shortly be called upon to undertake. You must hope on for a month, but at the end of that time you must accept the fact that I have handed my task over to the extremely capable hands of my comrades of the Royal Air Force as so many splendid fellows have already done. . . .

Though it will be difficult for you, you will disappoint me if you do not at least try to accept the fact dispassionately, for I shall have done my duty to the utmost of my ability. No man can do more, and no one calling himself a man could do less.

I have always admired your amazing courage in the face of continued setbacks; in the way you have given me as good an education and background as anyone in the country; and always kept up appearances without ever losing faith in the future. My death would not mean that your struggle has been in vain. Far from it. It means that your sacrifice is as great as mine. . . .

Today we are faced with the greatest organized challenge to Christianity and civilization that the world has ever seen, and I count myself honored to be the right

age and fully trained to throw my full weight into the
scale. For this I have to thank you. Yet there is more
work for you to do. The home front will still have to
stand united for years after the war is won. . . .

You must not grieve for me, for if you really believe
in religion and all that it entails that would be hypocrisy.
I have no fear of death. . . . I would have it no other
way. The universe is so vast and so ageless that the life
of one man can only be justified by the measure of his
sacrifice. We are sent to this world to acquire a personality and a character to take with us that can never
be taken from us. . . .

I firmly and absolutely believe that evil things are
sent into the world to try us; they are sent deliberately
by our Creator to test our mettle because He knows what
is good for us. The Bible is full of cases where the easy
way out has been discarded for moral principles.

. . . I consider my character fully developed. Thus
at my early age my earthly mission is already fulfilled and I am prepared to die with just one regret, and
one only—that I could not devote myself to making your
declining years more happy by being with you; but you
will live in peace and freedom and I shall have directly
contributed to that, so here again my life will not have
been in vain.
                              Your loving son. . . .

Are the sentiments expressed in this letter unusual? No, I think that they are typical of all sincere believers in God, and observers of God's Commandments. An American soldier who fell at Chateau Thierry in 1918 wrote the same thought as a paraphrase of that program of life expressed in the words: "I shall work as if everything depends on me. I shall pray since everything depends on God." Martin Treptow said: "America must win this war. Therefore, I will work, I will save, I will sacrifice, I will endure. I will fight cheerfully and do my utmost, as if the whole struggle depended on me alone."

III

All that I express here and all that I pray for Americans and for our country are summarized in a poem written by a priest of the Congregation of the Holy Cross, Father Gerald Fitzgerald:

A PRAYER FOR VICTORY

Lord, give us Victory!

Over our enemies in so much as they are Your enemies;

Over ourselves because we are Your sons who acknowl-
edge Your Paternity;

Over our meaner, baser selves, lest Victory over others

should lead us to ultimate defeat of that which is
noblest in us.

Lord, give us Victory;
Over injustice in international relations;
Over corruption in public life, that there may be a last-
    ing foundation upon which to erect Victory's tem-
    ples;
Over lack of integrity in private life;
Over selfishness in all life,
Lord, give us Victory.

Lord, give us Victory.
In clearer visioning of
    The mission of America;
    The glory of manhood;
    The achievement of paternity;
    The beauty of motherhood;
    The sacredness of childhood;
    The inviolability of our souls, our homes, our nation,
        our altars.

Lord, give us Victory;
Not alone in the might of our arms,
But in the righteousness of our cause,
The defense of the defenseless,

The succoring of the weak
The shackling of Injustice, Greed and Passion;
Lord, give us Victory.

Lord, give us Victory.
In the binding of all wounds;
The healing of all grievances;
The elimination of all injustices;
The exaltation of Peace;
The submission of all wills to Thy Holy Will.
Lord, give us Victory in Thy Son's Holy Name.

CHAPTER ELEVEN

The Road to Victory

A THOUSAND YEARS of history roll backwards and forwards before our bewildered gaze and stun us with the implications of the years that lie ahead. Sacred promises are broken; moral laws are in contempt; human life is cheap.

Since August 24, 1939, when the Holy Father, armed only with the "Sword of the Spirit," standing alone above public disputes and passions, appealed for peace by force of reason and justice and not by force of arms, petitions for peace have been offered at all Masses throughout the world. President Roosevelt appealed again and again for reason to prevail over madness, for justice to supplant hate and for charity to supersede greed. Their desires and efforts were in vain. However, on that account we are not to be defeatists in faith, hope and charity. We are not to be defeatists in religion.

Has religion been tried? I think not. It has been throttled, trampled, threatened, thwarted and thrust aside by ruthless, intellectually proud, morally bankrupt, power-greedy leaders. God has been excluded from the councils of nations and any universal norm of morality in the lives of individuals and society has been rejected. Even the voice of nature, the finger of God writing on the tablet of the human heart proclaims such fundamental postulates as that it is wrong to kill, to steal and to lie, procedures that are very much in vogue today.

So I say let us try religion, let us try religious living and let us try it on ourselves. It is not enough for us to wish and to expect our neighbor to love God and keep His commandments. We must first look to ourselves.

II

It will be a long time before the world will be tranquil again. Some countries have been destroyed by fifth columns and Trojan horses and America has centipede columns and whole stables of Trojan horses. Against them we must be on guard for the fight for freedom is never permanently won. To maintain freedom in America we must respect the rights of others to freedom. But, we must not grant so much freedom to others that they enslave us and destroy our beloved country.

It is not alone our fighting men who must sacrifice. It is all of us and all of us together. All our man-power, military, industrial and agricultural, our resources and our resourcefulness, fused together by our moral power, will not fail, cannot fail to bring us victory.

What will it profit us, however, to emerge victorious over attacks from abroad if at the same time we do not preserve the ideals of democracy at home and their indispensable supports of religion and morality. The answer is: It will profit us nothing because democracy without the props of religion and morality collapses into anarchy and tyranny. The happiness of the individual and the well-being of the nation may be destroyed not alone by foreign enemies but also by the lack of practical religious living and a fundamental morality based on the Ten Commandments.

We have this faith in God expressed in the Magna Charta of our liberties and reaffirmed through our history. "Religion," said our Commander-in-Chief, President Roosevelt, "is the source of democracy and of international good faith." The nation is composed of individuals and the character of the national life of democracies, as long as they remain democracies, is determined by the common denominator of the moral and physical qualities of its citizens.

Thus it is essential that men and women in the service of the country, not alone in the armed forces, but in all branches of the government, and men, women and children in civil life think of God and obey the laws of God.

The abandonment of Christ and His teachings in personal life, in social life, in civic life and in international life has brought us to the end of the world we have known. The way back to peace with justice through victory is in the identical order—personal righteousness, social decency, civic morality and international probity. Will this come to pass in our generation? We do not know. But we do know that we Americans can do something about it in our own lives and in our relationships with others. Not alone do we believe in God, but we must act as if we believed in Him and not alone in the last gasps of life but every day throughout our lives.

A large proportion of Americans do not go to Church, large numbers do not pray to God. However, let us forget the past. Let us look to today. If we have been neglectful in the past, we can start to pray now.

III

America's morale draws its strength not alone from natural courage but also from a just cause and a just God.

We know the facts. We face a situation forced on us. We wanted no land. We committed no economic wrongs. We suppressed no civic liberties.

Our free press and free radio bring us the words of the leaders of the powers of darkness ranged against us, ofttimes false and sometimes ridiculous. The oppressed, suffering, deluded and eventually rebellious, defeated people of the nations ranged against us know nothing of the attitude of the United States except that they must know in their hearts that America is on the level and on the square. Their leaders cannot squelch that thought nor can they suppress the knowledge that America has been invariably victorious. And she will be victorious again, cost what it may.

IV

There is a phrase oft attributed to St. Augustine which is most forceful in its truth and eloquence and one which exactly describes the traditional American spirit of tolerence for the opinions of others. It states that there should be unity in essential things, liberty in non-essential things, and charity in all things.

This phrase has flashed into mind with great frequency of late as thoughts are concentrated on the welfare of our country. Americanism in its essentials is the Americanism proclaimed and defined by the Declaration of Independence and our Constitution. Unfortunately, however, some of the definitions of Americanism that we are hearing today would be definitions of treachery twenty or twenty-five years ago. Today there are Americans who protect themselves with the flag of our country for the purpose of destroying that for which it stands, who stretch the wings of the American Eagle to break them. There are appeals to protect individuals whose avowed purpose is to destroy the Constitution, to tear it apart, to overturn by force the government which we all love and for which we are all willing to give our lives, as our forefathers did before us.

Even though men have different national and racial origins, they may still live in peace with one another.

In a certain Trappist monastery there are men of thirteen different nationalities living in sanctity and harmony. One of these Trappists is a man from the colored race and another is a physician of the Jewish race. That monastery represents a true democracy, a miniature democracy, if you will, but a model democracy. How well it would be for the world if the principles lived and exemplified in that monastery could be extended so that more men would work together to honor God, where all would love God and serve Him, and where all would respect and live happily with their neighbor! Would that these principles might be applied in national life and also in international relations. If those principles do not prevail, if they are destroyed in any respect in our country, then there will be disaster. For example, if in essential things we have liberty instead of unity the result will be anarchy. Again if we are forced to unity in non-essential things, the result will be regimentation and tyranny. Therefore should we follow both in civic and in religious matters the principle: "In essential things, unity; in non-essential things, liberty; and in all things, charity."

V

In these crucial times, I can find no better crystallization of the correct attitude towards life and the problems that life presents to us than is expressed in these words of St. Paul: "The charity of Christ presseth us."

The great Apostle of the Gentiles proposes Christ's love for man as the urgent cause impelling us to reciprocate Christ's love by service in charity to the needy and afflicted members of His Mystical Body. The remembrance of Christ's love, therefore, is for the thoughtful Christian a divine source of inspiration and of grace to answer the many demands for charity and for charitable services that come to us in our existence today.

The love of Christ for us creates love in us for Christ. Christ's charity elicits our corresponding charity. We know full well that no sacrifice asked of us is commensurate with the sacrifice that Jesus, the Son of God, has made for us and for our eternal salvation. In sacrifice as in all other things, the creature cannot equal the Creator, the earthly lover paragon the Love Divine.

Yet our inability to requite God's love does not, and cannot, dispense us from an earnest and courageous endeavor to prove our love for Christ in the precise manner in which He Himself has asked us to prove our affection. "If you love Me, keep My commandments." And again, "This is My Commandment, that you love one another as I have loved you."

Behold the qualification and the quality of our fraternal charity: "As I have loved you." We may judge our charity in the light of that degree of complete sacrifice that our Lord Himself has indicated—as He has loved us.

At the present hour in our lives, two great tasks confront us; two tasks, which, paradoxical though it may appear, must in their logical fulfillment be considered not only as compatible but as constituent parts of one full task.

One of these duties is the successful prosecution of

this war to final and ultimate victory. I do not think
I need to repeat that at the present time we are engaged in this war to maintain our existence. Nor do I
need to emphasize that charity tempered by justice and
the merciful defense of the helpless millions of numerous
enslaved nations constitute a Christian motivation for
war. It is a motive that impels us to move onward to victory, and a victory that shall not have within itself the
seeds of its own defeat. These seeds, hatred and revenge,
would bequeath to future generations only a heritage of
all the evils that have always followed in the wake of
war: ill-will, distrust, ignorance, distortion of historical
facts, selfishness, greed, cruelty and savagery. With such
camp-followers of war, there can be no real victory, no
real or final peace.

Ours, therefore, must be warfare on a higher plane;
a way that up to the present has brought us defeats at
the hands of treacherous, barbarous nations. These defeats, nevertheless, have left our national soul inviolate
because of our scrupulous adherence to national honor
and to our untiring and limitless efforts to promote national amities and to avoid war by appeals to human
reason and human hearts. In place of reason, however,
we found madness; in place of hearts, we found frozen
stones. The motivation for our warfare must be con-

sonant with the Christian ideals of charity, for thus will victory be assured, not only over the mighty might of our enemies but also over the souls of their righteous peoples.

If ever it were possible for a nation to fight out of a motive of charity to neighbor as well as for its own life, that possibility and that actuality are ours today. If ever we have looked for a deeper meaning in the stars and stripes of our flag, the white of justice and the red of charity, we know we have found it today. Every moment, every drop of blood and of sweat, every hour of fatiguing labor, every wound of our poor, torn humanity can and must be consecrated today to the defense of our country and the cause of charity, which is ultimately God's cause.

We have dedicated ourselves to the awful struggle that devolves on us as a nation and a people. We have given to our country not only an allegiance, but a conse-crated allegiance; not only a loyalty, but a consecrated loyalty; not only a service, but a service that draws its deepest significance and its greatest strength from God.

We of America fight today not only for human values, but also for those that are divine. It is true that our past has not been unsullied. In the pursuit of our inalienable rights to "life, liberty and the pursuit of happiness," we have certainly exaggerated the "pursuit of happiness" and distorted its meaning. Our lives at times have been

selfish lives and some interpretations of liberty have unjustly encroached on the liberty of others. But despite our
weaknesses and our mistakes, America's contemporary
position for international rectitude, for international justice, for international generosity, is unparalleled in
history.

From her founding fathers, America received a human
charter that has a divine sanction and implies a divine
destiny. It is a consecrated America which we wish to
preserve upon this earth, for which we fight and to which
we give our consecrated service. We place our patriotism
on the strong base of religion. For us the love of country
is not a house built upon the shifting sands of revolutionary change, but a house built upon a rock, which is God.

Individual characters are the components of national
character, and, as moral values are joined to democratic
values, America grows strong, America prepares for
victory.

St. Paul gives us the formula for victory. It must be
achieved in Christ—"they who live may not now live to
themselves, but unto Him who died for them and rose
again." We must "put on Christ." We cannot hope to
achieve the victory of peace with justice for our fellowmen until we as individuals have achieved victory in our
own souls. This is our first and foremost duty. This is the

achievement upon which the character of our contribution to the larger scope of victory depends. This is the victory for which each individual is personally responsible and on the attainment of which his salvation depends.

As Americans, we proclaim the common necessity of the defense of our beloved country. We shall never see her enslaved. We shall never see the sacred heritage of liberty torn from her, the democratic forms of government shorn from her. And the best way to preserve our country strong and free, the fundamental basis of all victory, is the upbuilding of the citizen as an individual, as a man who knows God and keeps God's commandments. This is the best and essential contribution that each of us can make to the winning of the war, the re-establishment of peace and the gaining of true liberties for all peoples.

VI

Praying to God to bless us all, with prayers for peace among nations and peace among men, I close with the prayer attributed to St. Francis of Assisi:

Lord, make me an instrument of Thy peace!
Where there is hatred . . . let me sow love.
Where there is injury . . . pardon.

Where there is doubt . . . faith.

Where there is despair . . . hope.

Where there is darkness . . . light.

Where there is sadness . . . joy.

O Divine Master, grant that I may not so much seek

To be consoled . . . as to console,

To be understood . . . as to understand,

To be loved . . . as to love;

                              for

It is in giving . . . that we receive;

It is in pardoning . . . that we are pardoned;

It is in dying . . . that we are born to eternal life.

THE END

GTU Library
2400 Ridge Road
Berkeley, CA 94709
For renewals call (510) 649-2500
All items are subject to recall.